THE CREATION MEMOS

GEOFFREY ATKINSON

WILLOW BOOKS
COLLINS
8 GRAFTON STREET
LONDON W1
1983

WILLOW BOOKS
WILLIAM COLLINS SONS & CO LTD
LONDON · GLASGOW · SYDNEY
AUCKLAND · TORONTO · JOHANNESBURG

FIRST PUBLISHED IN GREAT BRITAIN 1983
© GEOFFREY ATKINSON 1983

ATKINSON, GEOFFREY
THE CREATION MEMOS.
I. TITLE
823'.914 [F] PR6051.T/

ISBN 0 00 218012 X

PRINTED IN GREAT BRITAIN BY WILLIAM COLLINS SONS & CO LTD
GLASGOW

DESIGN: PENGILLEY DESIGNS
PHOTOGRAPHY: BASEMENT

IN THE BEGINNING THERE WAS

...a memorandum

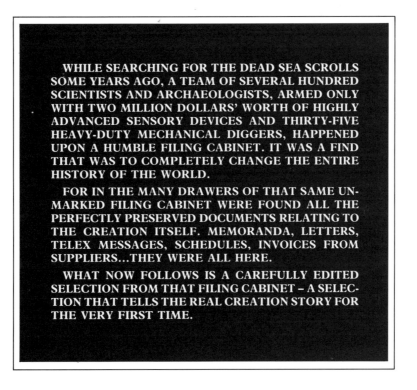

WHILE SEARCHING FOR THE DEAD SEA SCROLLS SOME YEARS AGO, A TEAM OF SEVERAL HUNDRED SCIENTISTS AND ARCHAEOLOGISTS, ARMED ONLY WITH TWO MILLION DOLLARS' WORTH OF HIGHLY ADVANCED SENSORY DEVICES AND THIRTY-FIVE HEAVY-DUTY MECHANICAL DIGGERS, HAPPENED UPON A HUMBLE FILING CABINET. IT WAS A FIND THAT WAS TO COMPLETELY CHANGE THE ENTIRE HISTORY OF THE WORLD.

FOR IN THE MANY DRAWERS OF THAT SAME UN-MARKED FILING CABINET WERE FOUND ALL THE PERFECTLY PRESERVED DOCUMENTS RELATING TO THE CREATION ITSELF. MEMORANDA, LETTERS, TELEX MESSAGES, SCHEDULES, INVOICES FROM SUPPLIERS...THEY WERE ALL HERE.

WHAT NOW FOLLOWS IS A CAREFULLY EDITED SELECTION FROM THAT FILING CABINET – A SELEC-TION THAT TELLS THE REAL CREATION STORY FOR THE VERY FIRST TIME.

AMALGAMATED WORLDS Pty

BIGGEST IN THE UNIVERSE

AMALGAMATED WORLDS PTY
AMALGAMATED WORLDS CORPORATION HOUSE
AMALGAMATED WORLDS CORPORATION PLAZA
AMALGAMATED WORLDS CORPORATION AVENUE
AMALGAMATED WORLDS CORPORATION VILLE

TELEPHONE: 964359214 to 954359792 (inclusive)
TELEX: AMALWORLDS

MINUTES OF LAST MEETING

1. New company cars for all directors — *Memo to self*

2. New company cars for all directors' wives — *Memo to wife*

3. Directors' toilet to be refurbished and modernised

4. Directors' car park to be refurbished and modernised

5. Directors' car park to be carpeted

6. Directors' car park to incorporate chandelier — *(A nice one with lots of dangling bits and a nice lot of bulbs)*

7. Directors' car park to incorporate sign at entrance that says 'Directors' Car Park' in big letters

8. Sign also to say 'Private' in big letters too

9. And 'Entrance in use Day and Night' in slightly bigger letters underneath

10. All directors' offices to be refurbished

11. All directors' offices to have 'Director's Office' on door

12. All directors' offices to have new doors *and door handles, + the bits that the door handles go into*

13. Even those that don't really need new doors

14. Directors' dining room to have a sign saying 'Directors' Dining Room' on the door

15. Sign to be in really big posh letters — *Brass — must be polished every day. Memo to cleaners!!*

16. Sign to be prominently displayed

17. All staff to be circulated about the new sign —

18. Directors' salaries to be increased by 500 per cent — *Memo required!*

19. Employees not to be told directors' salaries increased by 500 per cent

20. Employees to be told directors' salaries not increased for fourth year running

21. Employees to be told directors continuing to make great personal sacrifices for the company

22. Employees disputing this fact to be shot — *Check with legal dept.*

23. Brand new world to be created

*** *** ***
ACTION REQUIRED

Directors
R.V. Goldstein, B.M. Cohen, B.M.V. Schmidstein,
D.F.C. Rubenstein, R.F. Goldschmidt, T.G. Cohen-Cohen,
A.N.O.T.P.K.L. Freiburger, B.K. Jacobstein, H.L. Samuels

AMALGAMATED WORLDS Pty
BIGGEST IN THE UNIVERSE

AMALGAMATED WORLDS PTY
AMALGAMATED WORLDS CORPORATION HOUSE
AMALGAMATED WORLDS CORPORATION PLAZA
AMALGAMATED WORLDS CORPORATION AVENUE
AMALGAMATED WORLDS CORPORATION VILLE

TELEPHONE: 964359214 to 954359792 (inclusive)
TELEX: AMALWORLDS

Dear God,

At a recent meeting it was agreed by the Board of Amalgamated
Worlds that the company would consider the possibilities of
capital investment in the World market.

As our sole agent for the area considered for the project, we
were wondering if you would provide an estimate and feasibility
study for the project. The Board was keen to leave you with as
free a hand as possible and were prepared to accept your most
considered suggestions.

Needless to say, this is a matter of utmost confidentiality and
on no account should it be raised with any third party not
immediately involved. The fees will be commensurate with your
labours.

Yours sincerely,

T.G. Cohen-Cohen

T.G. Cohen-Cohen
Project Development Officer

Directors
R.V. Goldstein, B.M. Cohen
D.F.C. Rubenstein, R.F. Goldso
A.N.O.T.P.K.L. Freiburger, B.

"GOD"
CREATIVE CONSULTANCY PROPERTY SERVICING
Agent for: AMALGAMATED WORLDS Pty.
Registered Office: UNIT 4, LEVEL 2, CENTRAL PLAZA
Telephone: 353 500000 Telex: GOD
Directors: GOD (Managing, Sales, Financial)

Dear Mr. Cohen-Cohen,

Please accept my apologies for not replying sooner but
I have only recently returned from holidays.

The project you mentioned is indeed one to which I myself
had given much consideration and have felt long overdue.
Indeed, over lunch last week a number of business colleagues
had raised the very same topic and all had agreed upon its
wisdom. At a recent cocktail party I attended, the host -
an eminent accountant and good friend - announced that the
wisest investment for one's labours was in the World market
and said that anyone with the opportunity should 'get a
piece of the action', to use his expression.

Be assured that I will give the matter my most urgent
consideration.

Yours sincerely,

Veronica Makepiece

Veronica Makepiece

Dictated by God and signed in his absence

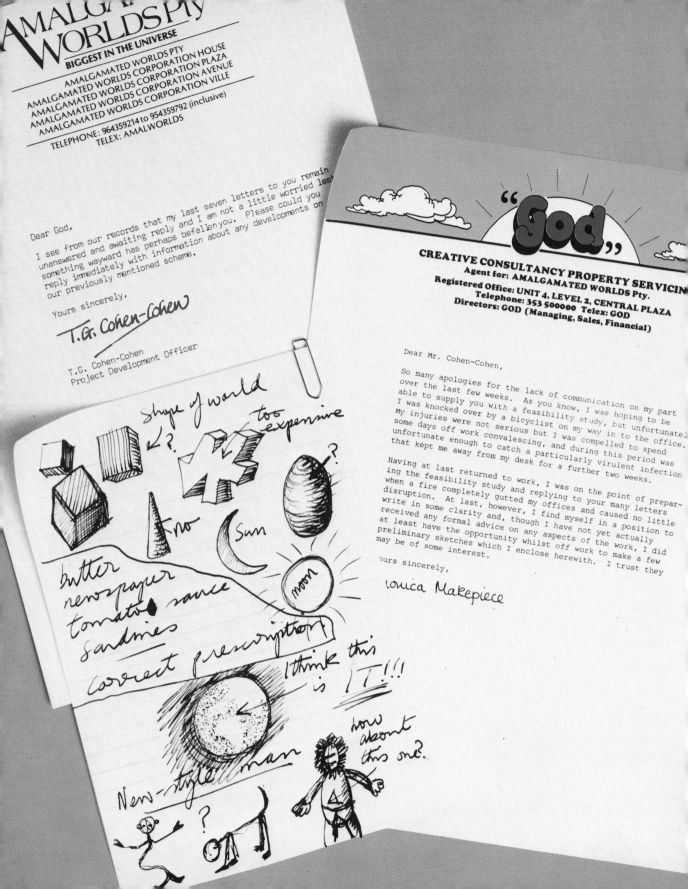

AMALGAMATED WORLDS Pty

BIGGEST IN THE UNIVERSE

AMALGAMATED WORLDS PTY
AMALGAMATED WORLDS CORPORATION HOUSE
AMALGAMATED WORLDS CORPORATION PLAZA
AMALGAMATED WORLDS CORPORATION AVENUE
AMALGAMATED WORLDS CORPORATION VILLE

TELEPHONE: 964359214 to 954359792 (inclusive)
TELEX: AMALWORLDS

Dear God,

I see from our records that my last seven letters to you remain unanswered and awaiting reply and I am not a little worried lest something wayward has perhaps befallen you. Please could you reply immediately with information about any developments on our previously mentioned scheme.

Yours sincerely,

T.G. Cohen-Cohen

T.G. Cohen-Cohen
Project Development Officer

"GOD"

CREATIVE CONSULTANCY PROPERTY SERVICING
Agent for: AMALGAMATED WORLDS Pty.
Registered Office: UNIT 4, LEVEL 2, CENTRAL PLAZA
Telephone: 353 500000   Telex: GOD
Directors: GOD (Managing, Sales, Financial)

Dear Mr. Cohen-Cohen,

So many apologies for the lack of communication on my part over the last few weeks. As you know, I was hoping to be able to supply you with a feasibility study, but unfortunately I was knocked over by a bicyclist on my way in to the office. My injuries were not serious but I was compelled to spend some days off work convalescing, and during this period was unfortunate enough to catch a particularly virulent infection that kept me away from my desk for a further two weeks.

Having at last returned to work, I was on the point of preparing the feasibility study and replying to your many letters when a fire completely gutted my offices and caused no little disruption. At last, however, I find myself in a position to write in some clarity and, though I have not yet actually received any formal advice on any aspects of the work, I did at least have the opportunity whilst off work to make a few preliminary sketches which I enclose herewith. I trust they may be of some interest.

Yours sincerely,

Veronica Makepiece

---

shape of world ←?

too expensive

?

butter
newspaper
tomato sauce
sandwich

Sun

moon

correct prescription?

I think this is IT!!!

New-style man

?

how about this one?

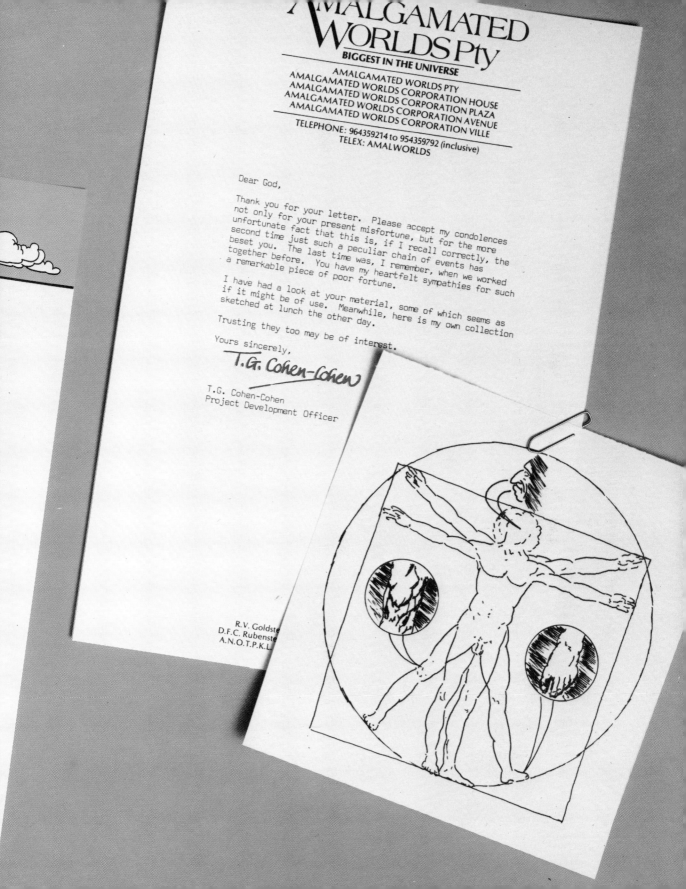

AMALGAMATED WORLDS Pty
BIGGEST IN THE UNIVERSE

AMALGAMATED WORLDS PTY
AMALGAMATED WORLDS CORPORATION HOUSE
AMALGAMATED WORLDS CORPORATION PLAZA
AMALGAMATED WORLDS CORPORATION AVENUE
AMALGAMATED WORLDS CORPORATION VILLE

TELEPHONE: 964359214 to 954359792 (inclusive)
TELEX: AMALWORLDS

Dear God,

Thank you for your letter. Please accept my condolences not only for your present misfortune, but for the more unfortunate fact that this is, if I recall correctly, the second time just such a peculiar chain of events has beset you. The last time was, I remember, when we worked together before. You have my heartfelt sympathies for such a remarkable piece of poor fortune.

I have had a look at your material, some of which seems as if it might be of use. Meanwhile, here is my own collection sketched at lunch the other day.

Trusting they too may be of interest.

Yours sincerely,

T.G. Cohen-Cohen

T.G. Cohen-Cohen
Project Development Officer

R.V. Goldste...
D.F.C. Rubenste...
A.N.O.T.P.K.L...

"GOD"

CREATIVE CONSULTANCY PROPERTY SERVICING
Agent for: AMALGAMATED WORLDS Pty.
Registered Office: UNIT 4, LEVEL 2, CENTRAL PLAZA
Telephone: 353 500000 Telex: GOD
Directors: GOD (Managing, Sales, Financial)

Dear Mr. Cohen-Cohen,

In connection with the project we are at present considering, I have recently been seeking the advice of a number of business colleagues and acquaintances. You may rest assured that I was most discreet in this endeavour, and was sure not to mention your company's name. I think you will find the replies informative.

Incidentally, my secretary informs me that we appear to have lost a sheet of notepaper on which I had drafted out a letter to my tax inspector regarding an overdue amount I would appear to owe. I know that you yourself are enlightened in these matters but I do fear that certain other parties reading the letter might regard some of the terms used therein as gravely offensive. A number of rather hastily drawn sketches to illustrate the points in the letter were attached, and I am naturally anxious that the correspondence should not fall into the wrong hands. I was wondering if the contents of this rather sensitive document had been sent to you inadvertently. If so, I wonder if you might return them to me as soon as possible.

With many thanks,

Veronica Makepiece

PP. God

Enclosu

ARNOLD GRIMP'S
ARNOLD GRIMP'S
ARNOLD GRIMP'S
ARNOLD GRIMP'S
| Interstellar Pet Emporium & Leathergoods |
ARNOLD GRIMP'S
ARNOLD GRIMP'S

Dear God,

I am afraid I cannot be of much assistance to you. We operate a small pet shop with only a limited stock of chiefly domesticated household pets and it would be impossible to supply you with all the animals you list in your 37-page letter, or even to hazard a guess at the price of same. Indeed, I'm somewhat at a loss as to exactly what you require. For instance, when you state 'Two Big Elephants (Male and Female)', are you thinking of the domesticated or the non-domesticated kind? The latter is cheaper but is apt to cause the most enormous problems, if you take my meaning.

I should think we could stock you with a very limited supply of cats, dogs, terrapins and budgerigars for around fifty dollars. But beyond that I would not care to offer a price.

Yours sincerely,

Agnes Grimp

A. P. Grimp
PP Manager

CONSOLIDATED
WEALTH & PROPERTY
Insurance Advisers and Brokers

Dear God,

Thank you for your letter concerning the proposed insurance for a new planet you intend to build. May I first thank you for allowing us to quote on this project, and may I also take the opportunity to wish you every success in the venture.

I see from your letter that you are interested in a policy that will cover the full cost of rebuilding should the 'world' be smitten in some way. This would naturally cover proportionate costs for partial rebuilding in the case of repairable damage. Without seeing the property concerned it is difficult to hazard a guess at the work involved and I fear you may be unduly optimistic when you suggest rebuilding should take one man only six days. In my own experience the average workman would barely have time to make his brew of tea in that period, but that is perhaps a slightly churlish view.

I would also point out that, even if it were possible to create a world in such a short period, you ought not to neglect the ever-increasing cost of raw materials. Don't underestimate the cost of items such as rivers and mountains!

Add to this the fact that you intend to populate the earth with a number of 'creatures'. All these would undoubtedly need personal insurance. And then there is the question of this 'man' you intend to create. Even covering him for third party, fire and theft would be expensive.

Frankly I doubt whether you'd get away with an annual premium of less than six million dollars a year.

To answer your other point, I doubt that you will convince any insurer to class your world as a 'vehicle' and I would immediately abandon any hope of qualifying for a no-claims discount.

Perhaps you could pop into the office next time you're in the neighbourhood and we could discuss the project. There are a number of potentially cost-saving ideas you might like to consider. For instance, if the world was registered as a charity you would be able to claim a substantial discount on any premium paid.

Incidentally, I should warn you that the final point you mention in your letter is known in the trade as 'fraud' and claiming for a world that never was is highly illegal. We would not be party to such a scheme and would beg you seriously to reconsider the matter.

Yours sincerely,

Denis Prick
Director
Consolidated Wealth & Property

Intergalactic Garden Centre
House Plants and Ecosystems
Our Speciality

Dear God,

　　Thank you for your letter concerning your proposed new planet. We would of course be delighted to help you stock your 'Garden of Eden', and would strongly recommend you contact us before proceeding with any plans. The false economy of not employing a specialist firm might well rebound badly when the final project is viewed and seen to be an ill-conceived disaster.

　　I see from your letter that you had considered using a number of plastic or 'synthetic' plants and trees, but I would certainly not recommend this. These types of plants do not 'breathe' as normal plants and in tropical and equatorial areas the heat from a forest made up of such trees would be truly oppressive. In addition, the 'bush fire' is often an integral part of much of the vegetation we supply, but if this fire were to be similarly applied to your plastic vegetation, one could only assume the final outcome would be a revolting swamp of molten plastic.

　　Nor would we recommend the other suggestion you make, viz. covering the whole thing over with concrete. Of course, as gardeners, we are naturally biased in this matter. But if one is realistic, a giant concrete-clad ball would not look particularly attractive, nor would it offer much of a home for the 'abundant creatures that do give forth and multiply', which I see you intend to house there. I dare say there wouldn't be much multiplying under such exposed conditions.

　　As a general rule, I would suggest a mixture of grass, trees, shrubs, and all that 'do bear seed and give forth and multiply by the seed'.

　　We would of course be happy to advise you further nearer the time.

Yours sincerely,

Nigel Creep-Quietly
Sales Manager

Superfab
Superior Fabrics Ltd.
Consultants in Interior and Exterior Designs

Dear God,

    Thank you for writing to us at Superfab with regard to decoration of your forthcoming world.

    We must, I fear, point out that our first-hand experience in the decoration of such a large object as a world is a tiny bit limited. And while we could make any number of super suggestions based on our long and intimate knowledge of home decor, if these were to be applied on a larger scale to your proposed world then there is a grave danger of mistakes occurring and the whole episode ending in tears.

    For instance, the bold use of pattern and fabrics which can so often enliven a small or dark nook would surely be inappropriate for the vast amount of land you are considering. And <u>do</u> try to avoid thermo-plastic tiles. Quite apart from the labour that would be involved in tiling such a colossal object, you must appreciate that the maintenance would be virtually impossible. If I were you, I'd go for a little something in a plain woollen twist that requires naught but a quick dab with the vacuum cleaner and an occasional shampoo.

    In the circumstances, I can only advise you to go for a pale or neutral tone for the vertical and facing subjects, and a good quality woollen carpet for any flat surfaces. And don't go anywhere <u>near</u> flock wallpaper. Take my advice: it would be totally unsuited to this kind of work. Unless you want it to look like a gigantic Indian restaurant.

                Yours sincerely,

                Ted Nibber

                Ted Nibber
                Customer Liaison Dept.
                Superfab

Rich, Richer & Richest
CHARTERED ACCOUNTANTS

Dear God,

Thank you for your letter referring to the new planet you
intend to build. I admit the tax position is not clear.

You should not be liable for VAT on the new world, nor on
the labour employed in creating such a world. However,
any income derived from the project would certainly be liable
for tax. If, for instance, you were thinking of charging
rent for living on earth this ought to be borne in mind.
But don't forget that legitimate expenses such as heating
and lighting could under these circumstances be taken into
account.

I note from your letter that you intend to build the entire
world in six days and would point out that, from a financial
point of view, you might care to have your income for this
work assessed over a three-year period. I would also advise
you to consider the timing of this period. By deferring
some of the creation until the next financial year you should
be able to save yourself a considerable amount of tax.

I'm afraid your suggestion of 'not telling all those creatures
that creepeth down at the tax office anything about it' is
somewhat naive. The taxman is a pretty shrewd customer and
would be sure to catch up with you eventually. However, you
might like to consider the possibility of setting the whole
thing up as a public limited company and issuing shares. This
would certainly limit your personal tax liability and might
well reduce the overall tax bill. As a company you would
qualify for certain extra benefits, and if you were to select
an improvement zone for the site you might well avoid tax
altogether.

Finally, I am returning your blank cheque herewith. I appreciate
the sentiments involved but I'm afraid the taxman is unlikely
to regard unsolicited offers of money in a favourable light.

I trust the advice may be of assistance to you in your project.

Yours sincerely,

C. Dull

Colin Dull
Partner
Rich, Richer and Richest

Dear God,

Thank you for your letter. It does indeed seem a long time since we played golf together! Perhaps we could get together one Saturday for a few holes. Do phone.

As to your request, let me say that I'm not altogether familiar with the area to which you refer and a fair price will always depend on site. However, I would say the figure you quote is not far off the mark, especially if as you say it is an up-and-coming area.

For advice on items to be aware of, my best tip would be to have a quiet word with the neighbours. They can usually offer an invaluable source of local knowledge. And do look out for any Black Holes. Too many people build worlds on or near Black Holes, only to see them disappear into oblivion within a few weeks.

Don't forget about that game of golf!

Best wishes,

Leroy del Schwartzdigger

Leroy del Schwartzdigger
<u>Partner</u>

"GOD"

CREATIVE CONSULTANCY PROPERTY SERVICING
Agent for: AMALGAMATED WORLDS Pty.
Registered Office: UNIT 4, LEVEL 2, CENTRAL PLAZA
Telephone: 353 500000 Telex: GOD
Directors: GOD (Managing, Sales, Financial)

Dear Mr. Cohen-Cohen,

Re: World (The), Creation of

Please find enclosed legal advice from my solicitors, who have
kindly advised me as to the legal aspects pertaining to the
above project.

As you will see, it does appear to be a particularly cumbersome
and involved matter. However, I am confident that, with a little
thought, the difficulties mentioned can be successfully overcome.
Trusting then that the enclosed will be of interest.

Yours sincerely,

Veronica Makepi...

pp. God

Enclosures

CROOKED & BENT
Solicitors, Commissioners for Oaths, Licensed Betting Shop

Dear Mr. God,

Re: Creation of World Project

I have studied your letters. And drawings. How talented you are!
And what an eye for colour. I would never have thought to use orange and
green for such a project. How unusual.

I fear, however, that I must dampen this enthusiasm for the avant garde
slightly and beg you to consider the legal implications of the work you
intend to undertake.

Firstly, let me point out that legally you are obliged to adhere
to all planning rules and regulations. I agree with your quaint adage that
'actions speak louder than words'. But when those words are written into
legal documents, and when those legal documents are in the hands of
important people, then it is as well to at least consider what they say.
What's more, while you personally - and I quote - 'could not give a
monkeys' about town and country planning, I fear other people with considerable influence could, and will be sure to, give you a rough time of it in
the not too distant future.

Let me therefore outline the legal position for your information:

(1) Planning Permission All new worlds, and extensions to
all existing worlds, must receive full planning permission
and must be built in accordance with any relevant bye-laws.
You should submit plans, stating all relevant dimensions
and all construction substances to be used. You should also
enclose a sworn statement of intent as to the use of the
property (this is mainly to avoid sub-letting).

(2) Health and Safety You must notify the Health and Safety
executive of the appropriate area as to your intention to
build a new world. And you should ensure they are
furnished with all necessary information. In particular,
they will wish to know whether the world is to have correct
sanitation (a particularly important aspect since I see
that you intend to instal camels). And they will wish to
be made aware of any smells that might be expected to
emanate from the world (again, I come back to the camels).
Remember that with a world of this size you will be legally
required to provide a minimum number of toilets and a minimum number of wash hand basins. There is, incidentally, no
maximum number.

(3) Registration As owner of a new world you will be required
to register the same with the Land Registry. You should b...

(continued)

God

sure to state your full name and address on the documents
with which you will be furnished. And your occupation.
And the full name and address of the world. The require-
ment to give your inside leg measurement has now been
removed from all forms.

(4) <u>Fire</u> You are legally required, in all worlds intended for
multiple occupancy by more than 12 people, to provide
adequate fire safety precautions, including fire escapes,
fire extinguishers, fire buckets, some shiny yellow trousers
and a rope. In addition, you must prove that the world is
constructed with non-combustible substances, in accordance
with the latest regulations. I enclose a list of these for
your reference.

(5) <u>Animals</u> Any animals you intend to keep on the world
should be inspected by a registered veterinary surgeon and
a certificate issued by the same. All animals will be
required to be kept in a reasonable manner and if you
intend to slaughter any, you must be sure to obtain planning
permission for an abattoir to be built. You should pay
particular attention to the official publication entitled
'Rules and Regulations For The Hacking Up of Dead and Half-
Dead Animals' published by the Office of Health and Safety.
This tells you how **you** may, or may not, butcher innocent
animals. (I've enclosed a copy of this, too.)

I would again stress most strongly that legally the owner of a new
world must satisfy a number of stringent requirements. Please do not
do anything foolish. Just because I am, to use your words, 'a well-
known and well-liked solicitor', it does not mean that I can get you
'off the hook, if you catch my drift'. The law is the law, and as a
solicitor I regret that it is my professional duty to abide by it.

Yours lawfully,

R. B. J. Fiddle
Very Senior Part...

RULES AND REGULATIONS
FOR THE HACKING UP
OF DEAD AND HALF-DEAD ANIMALS

(Being the complete regulations regarding the
wholesale butchery of innocent and harmless
animals with knives, saws, axes, meat
cleavers, boathooks and expensive heavy-duty
chain saws)

Published by
The Office of Health and Safety
(Massacre of Dead Animals Department)

Ref MROPLTH/4567/apl(1)(iii)

RECOMMENDED LIST OF ACCEPTED MATERIALS FOR USE IN CONSTRUCTING WORLDS

Sand

Water

Mud

Rocks

Bricks

More mud

Pilchards

Limestone

Dead pigeons

'Dead pigeon' flavour ice cream

Socks with holes in the toes

Dirty pillowcases

Grit

Margarine

Bacon, eggs, toast, and a small glass of orange juice

Old copies of The New York Times

Wood

Sewage

Used teabags

Cold soup that's gone off a bit

Empty Corn Flakes packets

Navel fluff

Unwanted body hair

Silt

Old paint brushes that you last used 10 years ago but have never got round
to throwing away because you thought that one day you just might find a
use for them

Those foam-backed carpet tiles which you used to have in the kitchen but
took up years ago because they kept slipping and causing you to trip but
which you swore you'd never throw away because they were still in quite
good nick and you never know when they might come in handy

AMALGAMATED WORLDS Pty
BIGGEST IN THE UNIVERSE

AMALGAMATED WORLDS PTY
AMALGAMATED WORLDS CORPORATION HOUSE
AMALGAMATED WORLDS CORPORATION PLAZA
AMALGAMATED WORLDS CORPORATION AVENUE
AMALGAMATED WORLDS CORPORATION VILLE

TELEPHONE: 964359214 to 954359792 (inclusive)
TELEX: AMALWORLDS

Dear God,

Am in receipt of your latest. At first sight I agree it doesn't look too promising! But at this stage I wouldn't be too pessimistic. Amalgamated Worlds, though I do say it myself, are a very large organisation; a very large organisation indeed. Even by the standards of other large organisations. And as a very large organisation we do have access to certain 'levers'. Bribery is not a word I like to use. But financial inducement is. Rest assured your solicitor's comments have been noted and respected but I feel there is still room for hope.

Meanwhile, I thought the enclosed calling cards might be of some use to you. I appear to have accumulated them over a number of years and only chanced upon them when I was clearing out my desk this week.

How is the feasibility study coming on? All here at Amalgamated Worlds are greatly looking forward to seeing the results. Or rather most of us are. There are still one or two members of the Board who view the whole thing with some scepticism, but most regard it, on the whole, with reasonable enthusiasm. Or at least not downright contempt.

How's the leg? When I phoned last week your secretary told me you'd torn some ligaments playing squash.

With good wishes,

Tracey Goldberg

PP T.G. Cohen-Cohen
Project Development Officer

Enclosures

GENETIC ENGINEERING LIMITED

For all your problems with MAN & WOMAN
Discreet Service Guaranteed
All Gynaecological Work Undertaken

Need a Continent in a Hurry?

BARRY BOLTON & SON

have just the answer!
Home-assembly Polystyrene Continents
(only 36 hrs to assemble)

QUAKES
FOR ALL YOUR EARTHQUAKE NEEDS
24-hour Service

fit all leading makes of continent

MUD, SILT, FLUVIAL DEPOSITS
RING GROT BROTHERS

We've been silting up rivers for 1000's of
years ... for all your braided drainage,
delta, and fluvial problems, ring GROT
BROTHERS!

New, Unusual, Exotic
Largest Stockist of Animals
Hundreds of Rare Animals in stock

TEBBITS

Available complete or self-assembly
All fully guaranteed

CONTINENTAL DRIFT A PROBLEM?

Try HOLTS "Polycont"
Our unique fibra-grip system
literally bonds continents together.
Avoids messy continental divide

DIMMOCK & THRUPP

Peninsular Specialists
All Makes – All Designs
Also: Tombolas, Spits & Ox-bow Lakes
Over 50,000,000,000 years' experience
Free Quote

CLOUDS
Choosing clouds to match can be difficult:
there are so many to choose from. But now
you can pay for only the clouds you use with

CLOUDSHARE INC.
(The fast-growing new concept in shared
ownership)

CREATIVE CONSULTANTS LTD

We provide a fully-comprehensive names service.
Names for everything!
Also gift pack of 250 unused names
Ideal for any feature!

TEDDY & KEITH ACROPOLIS

All types of climate

We can fit and install all leading types of
climate, or adapt existing climates to
meet your requirements.

Neat, clean! Prices on application

UPLIFT's

(Geological Uplift Unlimited)
"From mountains to molehills"
Send for free brochure and sample.

ALSO

Peneplains – we have all leading makes
of peneplain (residual, rejuvenated,
deeply eroded) available for
IMMEDIATE DESPATCH

Need a Qualified Geomorphologist?
'V', 'U' and Hanging Valleys.
All small contract work undertaken.

Will visit – No obligation.

CHEAP!   DUD STAMP

NO WORLD IS COMPLETE
WITHOUT A ROBINSON'S WHALE.
ROBINSON'S WHALES ARE THE
ONLY APPROVED MAKE FOR MOST
COUNCIL AND CONTRACT WORK.
WHEN CREATING A NEW WORLD
BE SURE TO ASK FOR

ROBINSON'S WHALES

LOOK FOR THE MARK ON THE

GRAVE-AN-IMAGE

Grave-An-Image have been hand-
creating quality men and women for
years, and can design to your specific
requirements, or submit designs for
approval.

WHEN YOUR RIVERS LOOK LIKE THIS,
YOU NEED UNBRAID Ltd.

Unbraid straighten rivers, remove
meanders and unbraid all braided
drainage, leaving a neat, clean and tidy
finish!
(Private and Contract Work Undertaken)

VOLCANOS, EARTHQUAKES

Choosing the *right* volcano or earthquake
can be very difficult – but not any more.
Because now there's a scientific solution:

COMPUTACATASTROPHE

Simply phone us with your requirements, and we
will put you in ... terally hundreds of
... a major catast...

TYROLLEAN UNLIMITED

Stockist of all leading makes of Tyrollean Life

Rustic Snow-capped Mountains,
Rustic Mountain Goats,
Rustic Mountain Pastures

EROSIAN & DENUDATION A PROBLEM?

Arthur Cooper
(Geomorphologist)

be pleased to advise and assist
normal commissions undertaken

SWAMPS
Ring us before you get
'BOGGED DOWN'

REAGAN & REAGAN

Swamp and mud suppli...

ANTIPODEAN ARTISTS
Acknowledged experts in all work 'Down
Under', including Koalas, Dingos and Sheilas!
New clients always welcome
ANTIPODEAN ARTISTS

NATURAL VEGETATION

24-Hour Service
Fast & Reliable
Botanic Service
offered by
BONA FIDE BOTANIST

Green & Pleasant

NOBBIES
Fastest Polar & Sub-polar Conversions
Permafrosting, Ice-capping, Glacial
Scenery
Stockists of Icebergs, Pack Ice, Glaciers,
etc.

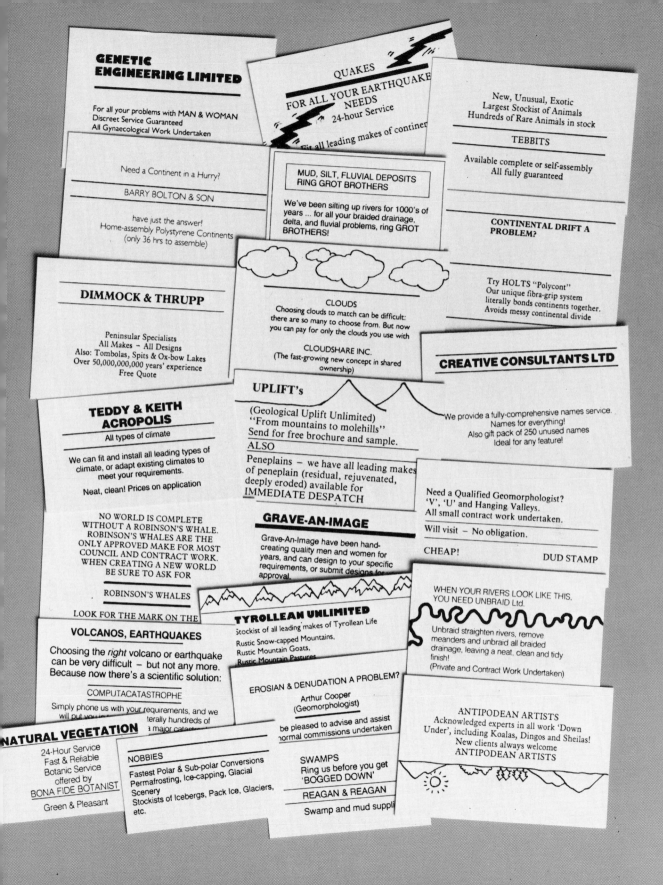

CREATIVE CONSULTANCY PROPERTY SERVICING
Agent for: AMALGAMATED WORLDS Pty.

Registered Office: UNIT 4, LEVEL 2, CENTRAL PLAZA
Telephone: 353 500000 Telex: GOD
Directors: GOD (Managing, Sales, Financial)

Dear Mr. Cohen-Cohen,

Re: Creation of A World

I am sorry that the feasibility study has not yet been forthcoming. I have been away from the office for some time with a severe attack of nasal colic. Rest assured I will now devote my energies to the task of obtaining the necessary study.

With kind regards,

Veronica Makepiece

God

AMALGAMATED WORLDS Pty
BIGGEST IN THE UNIVERSE

AMALGAMATED WORLDS PTY
AMALGAMATED WORLDS CORPORATION HOUSE
AMALGAMATED WORLDS CORPORATION PLAZA
AMALGAMATED WORLDS CORPORATION AVENUE
AMALGAMATED WORLDS CORPORATION VILLE

TELEPHONE: 9643592714 to 954359792 (inclusive)
TELEX: AMALWORLDS

My Dear God,

Re: Creation of A World

You may recall that some ten weeks ago we agreed that you
would arrange with an appropriate company to furnish me
with a feasibility study into the prospect of creating a
world.

I see from our records that this study is yet to be forthcoming and I wonder if you could look into the matter for
me.

Trusting you will report back at your earliest convenience.

Yours as ever,

T.G. Cohen-Cohen

T.G. Cohen-Cohen
Project Development Officer

Directors
R.V. Goldstein, B.M. Cohen, B.M.V. Schmidstein,
D.F.C. Rubenstein, R.F. Goldschmidt, T.G. Cohen-Cohen,
A.N.O.T.P.K.L. Freiburger, B.K. Jacobstein, H.L. Samuels

FROGGINS, FROGGINS & FROGGINS.
Consultants
and Business
Research

Dear God,

Re: Creation of World

Thank you for your letter. I regret, however, that we are unable to
help with your feasibility study. Our senior partner has recently
been struck down with a severe case of gout and, I fear, will not be
with us for some time, while I myself am suffering from a severe
case of dysentry that compels me to

High-quality
P·R·U·D·E·S
Research

Dear God,

Re: Creation of World

Your letter has been forwarded to me for reply. It is
with enormous relief that I am writing to tell you it will
not be possible for us to undertake the work you require.

May I say first of all that Prudes are high quality
researchers and not tax inspectors, a misconception under
which you appear to be labouring. After one quick look at
the crude and offensive drawings which you submitted to us, and
which I am returning under separate cover, I feel it is only
right that we invite you to go elsewhere. Some people might
consider the project you are planning to be interesting or
rewarding. A few might even regard it as having some merit. We,
I'm afraid, do not.

Quite apart from the unsavoury nature of the work envisaged,
it is also a technical impossibility. I have always held the
impression that you were slightly detached from reality and your
recent letter has only served to prove that my impressions were
correct.

Please do not contact me again. I am an honest, hard working
citizen and requests such as yours serve only to upset me.

Yours shakenly,

Brian H.M.V. Prude.

Brian H.M.V. Prude

N'S CON'S CON'S CON'S CON'S CON

**(Incorporating Consolidated Money,
Consolidated Wealth, Consolidated Bank Accounts,
Consolidated Bags of Loose Change)**

Dear God,

<u>Re: Creation Of A World</u>

Thank you for your request that we undertake a small feasibility study for you. Regretfully, we cannot oblige you. We are at present moving offices, our present accommodation having been mysteriously engulfed in a dreadful fire not a week ago. Luckily we had just had the good fortune to take out a substantial insurance policy and will not, I'm relieved to report, be financially burdened by the mishap.

It is ironical that, on the previous occasions you have been in touch with me, I have had to turn down your requests for similar reasons. What an amazing coincidence. It does appear that my ill-luck with fires and floods is matched only by my foresight in negotiating insurance cover!

Incidentally, were you yourself considering an unfortunate fire in the near future, I would be willing (for a small fee, of course) to supply you with the names and addresses of certain 'consultants' who would, I am sure, be able to satisfy your every need.

In the meantime, apologies again for the fact that we are unable on this occasion to offer you assistance. At least not until my wife and I return from our luxurious round-the-world cruise.

With all best wishes,

Aarfon Growbag.

Aarfon Growbag

PARKHURST PARTNERS
—"A nod's as good as a wink!"—

Dear God,

Re: Creation of A World

Thank you for your letter. What a pleasure it was to hear from you
after such a long time. And how very interesting - a new world. You
must be very excited. I fear though that we will not be in a position
to help you with your intended feasibility study. We have just recently
closed our 'property consultancy' office after a somewhat troublesome
enquiry by the local constabulary: an enquiry about which I feel
most bitter.

We are now, as it happens, in the process of opening a 'pre-owned
vehicle allocation agency' which I feel sure will prove to be a great
success. Perhaps you would like to call by when next in this manor.
We do from time to time find vehicles which have become unavoidably
separated from their owners and need a hasty reallocation, and I
feel sure we could find something to suit.

Trusting you are fit and well.

Yours dodgily,

Flash Stan & Fingers Picklock

Grump, Gromp, McCulloch
Research Partners

Dear God,

Your request for assistance has been received with shock
and dismay. Perhaps it has escaped your attention that settlement is required on no less than eight outstanding accounts,
and that legal action is pending on four of these.

I suggest that all sums be paid posthaste, if not sooner.
I'd like to take this opportunity to remind you that we are a
registered business, not a registered charity, and like all other
businesses depend upon prompt and early settlement of accounts
to remain solvent. You, for your part, seem to operate under
some totally different rules.

Until you mend your ways, we shall have no cause whatsoever
to discuss 'exciting new projects'. Other than in the Courts.

Yours sternly,

Lionel Gromp
Lionel Gromp

"God"

CREATIVE CONSULTANCY PROPERTY SERVICING
Agent for: AMALGAMATED WORLDS Pty.
Registered Office: UNIT 4, LEVEL 2, CENTRAL PLAZA
Telephone: 353 500000 Telex: GOD
Directors: GOD (Managing, Sales, Financial)

Dear Mr. Cohen-Cohen,

Re: Creation of World

Please find enclosed the feasibility study for the world. I very much regret it is not quite as I had envisaged it, but unfortunately every firm I contacted about the work seemed unable to render assistance. I was, alas, therefore compelled to use a company I have never dealt with before. Nor, might I add, will I ever deal with them again!

Please accept my most sincere apologies for what has turned out to be something well below the very high standards which I know you are keen to uphold. I do apologise. Profusely. And humbly. I can only trust that in your magnanimity you will see fit to accept these apologies in the spirit in which they are offered.

Yours grovellingly,

Veronica Makepiece

PP· God
(Sorry.)

Enclosures

CRUDE & OFFENSI
(Established 20 minutes ago.

Dear Mister God,
       Please find enclosed the study what you asked us to prepare . We're sorry it's ~~xxxxxx~~ a bit scruffy . But the cat got hold of it . Do'nt worry about the stains - that's only lard from the ball on the cat's bum.
Full settlement within 2½ days.

Your's truly,

R.S.J. Girder

We have been asked by our clients to advise as to the suitability of creating a new world, and would report accordingly:

1. We're not sure what <u>shape</u> would be best. But we think roundish would be O.K. Though maybe with a few corners. Or maybe not. But we think it should definitely be the shape you think it should be. Or if not, then it should be some other shape.

2. <u>Colour</u> We ~~xxjixji~~ would suggest a good colour be used. Preferably one that you think is good.

3. We would suggest you choose an appropriate <u>size</u> for the world. A sort of average-ish size, we think . Although it could maybe be a shade larger . Maybe you could have a few words with someone else and see what they think. Or what they would do if they were in your shoes. That's what we always do. Ask around . It saves a lot of bother. (Incidentally, that goes for the bit about colour too.)

4. <u>Surface</u> The world should definitely have a surface.

5. <u>Trees</u> The world should definitely have a few trees knocking around to make it look pretty (unless you don't agree).

6. <u>Acne</u> The world should not have acne.

7. <u>Trees with acne</u> The world should not have trees with acne. If they have acne then they are not proper trees and you've been sold a pup.

8. <u>Smell</u> The world shouldn't be too smelly, otherwise no one will want to live there. Except people who like living in smelly places. And let's face it, who wants that sort of person living on their world. Mind you, that's only our opinion.

That concludes our feasibility study. If there are any further questions then we wouldn't mind answering them. As long as they're not too difficult . And as long as they don't involve us actually having to write a reply.

AMALGAMATED WORLDS Pty

BIGGEST IN THE UNIVERSE

AMALGAMATED WORLDS CORPORATION HOUSE
AMALGAMATED WORLDS CORPORATION PLAZA
AMALGAMATED WORLDS CORPORATION AVENUE
AMALGAMATED WORLDS CORPORATION VILLE

TELEPHONE: 964359214 to 954359792 (inclusive)
TELEX: AMALWORLDS

Dear God,

I have recently returned to my office after several painful days off work with a severely ingrowing toenail and upon my return was presented with your most recent letter and enclosures.

I do indeed agree that the feasibility study was inadequate in all respects and have therefore found it necessary to take up your profound apology. I have incidentally taken the precaution of destroying the report before anyone here should read it and perhaps gain the impression that we were entertaining incompetency.

Meanwhile, might I suggest the work be put out to tender. At least this way we might obtain some indication of the possible cost. I have therefore requested a specification and draft tender be prepared and enclose herewith copies of same text for your reference.

With kind regards,

T.G. Cohen-Cohen

T.G. Cohen-Cohen
Project Development Of...

TENDERS

Tenders are hereby invited
for the Creation of
ONE WORLD

Ref: AMAL/WORL/

Amalgamated Worlds Pty are considering the possibilities of creating a brand new world-like structure and invite interested parties to submit full tenders for all aspects of the work on or before the last day of this month. All applicants should be fully conversant with world construction and have demonstrable skills to the same and be so prepared to carry out the required works to the specification of the full Bill of Works available on application. Site to be left in a reasonable and tidy manner.

Work to consist ONE WORLD of rock, sand and water construction, having orbic shape and estimated weight of 6,000,000,000,000,000,000,000 tons and volume of 250,000,000,000 cubic miles. Or thereabouts. DIMENSIONS AND AREA of the world should have girth not exceeding 25,000 miles and revolve about itself on a sealed, maintenance-free bearing. WORLD to incorporate regular orbital system with other planets and not requiring other such planets to be moved. Applicants should supply a separate design specification for separating waters and a plan using waters in a 2:1 relation with land to create a pleasing and acceptable series of continents. Design should include fullest range of currently accepted geographical features. Applicants will be further expected to include their intention for heating and lighting said world.

Sundry items Tenders should include full price and details for sundry items as detailed on the specification sheet and wherever so should specify all work to be contracted out with name of said contractor. Sundry items will include: DESERTS, PENINSULAS, MOUNTAINS, VOLCANOS, ANTS, CAVES, GLACIAL FEATURES, RIVERS, EARWIGS, LAKES, WATERFALLS, BADGERS ... and to include adequate provision for future development and/or modification to customer's requirements. Tenders should include price for a full range of fish and aquatic animals.

Man Tenders to include a separate price for the provision of a man and a woman to live on the world.

Lighting and heating Lighting is to be on an integral sun and moon system and should again provide for maintenance-free running. A convector system is preferred for all air circulation and tenders should wherever possible avoid quoting for conventional piped hot water.

Terms and conditions Preference will be given to tenders specifying the shortest possible period of construction. Applicants should also be prepared to issue 12-month guarantees on all parts and labour.

Further particulars and formal tenders should be submitted to:

GOD
Agent General
AMALGAMATED WORLDS PTY.
(Quoting Ref...

WO

	LABOUR
FIRST DAY	Divide light from darkness. Check light. Ensure it is good.
SECOND DAY	Install firmament device in mids of waters. Divide waters from waters (under firmament).
THIRD DAY	Gather together waters in one pl and dry out land. Fit grass, her and fruit tree yielding fruit af his kind. Ensure grass, and herb yielding seed, and the tree yiel fruit are in full working order.
FOURTH DAY	Instruct qualified person to fit days and seasons. Hang stars in firmament to give light upon the earth. Fit sun and moon.
FIFTH DAY	Install abundant moving creatures in accordance with customer's instructions
AY	Under customer's supervision che working order of creatures that things that creepeth one woman

RS	MATERIALS	TOTAL HOURS
	2 gross large nails 5 galls matt white emulsion 1 8' x 4' sheet plyboard 10 sheets sandpaper	8
	1.3×10^{18} tons water 5,882,000,000,000,000,000 tons earth 1 tube glue	$14\frac{1}{2}$
	125,000 species grass/herbs/fruit 267,000,000 tons potting compost 35,000 bottles fertiliser	$24\frac{1}{2}$
	6,000 stars 25,000 assorted brass hooks 25 metres string	$32\frac{1}{2}$
	74,000,000,000,000,000 moving creatures that hath life and fowl that may fly above the earth	$46\frac{1}{2}$
	59,000,000,000,000,000 assorted animals and creepy-crawlies 1 man } to be supplied 1 woman }	63
	Nil	63

ABBREVIATED SPECIFICATION SHEET

Tenders should include full price for the following:

Dividing light from darkness
Firmament (one)
Dividing waters (under firmament)
Gathering together waters
Gathering together dry land in one place
Bringing forth grass, herb yielding seed and fruit, tree yielding fruit after its kind whose seed is in itself, upon the earth
Installing light
Installing gas and electricity
Installing 13 amp plug sockets
Dividing day, years, seasons (to customer's instructions)
Making stars (two gross)
Bringing forth many creatures that hath life (abundant)
Bringing forth fowl that may fly above the earth in the open firmament of heaven
Creating whales, living creatures, winged fowl (after their kind)
Creating lots of quiet little coves with sandy beaches
Creating funny little bits of land that stick out into the sea
Creating other bits of land that look as though they're going to fall down at any minute
Creating nice places for picnics
Ensuring creatures multiply and fill the waters and the sea
Bringing forth cattle, creeping things, beasts of the earth, and hamsters
Creating man
From rib of man create one woman (subject to availability)

"god"

CREATIVE CONSULTANCY PROPERTY SERVICING
Agent for: AMALGAMATED WORLDS Pty.
Registered Office: UNIT 4, LEVEL 2, CENTRAL PLAZA
Telephone: 353 500000 Telex: GOD
Directors: GOD (Managing, Sales, Financial)

Dear Mr. Cohen-Cohen,

I received by post today the first selection of prices for
'The World'.

I must confess they have worked out a little more expensive
than I had first envisaged. And a little less suitable. In
fact, a lot less suitable. It does seem that our brief has
been universally ignored by all the parties concerned. Not
that it is for me to cast aspersions; I am not a builder. But
I would suggest that some of the companies applying for the
work might be best advised directing their efforts elsewhere.
Indeed, these were very much the points I made in my strongly
worded letter to the National Builders Council. If the
building trade cannot train sufficient young men capable of
supplying a realistic price for such a simple job as a creation,
then we are in a pretty sorry state.

I have enclosed the estimates for your inspection. I fear
you will find little there of encouragement.

Yours in haste,

Veronica Makepiece

PP. God

Enclosures

EXOTIC WORLDS

ESTIMATE

We have pleasure in supplying our price for your recently advertised
project and would advise you of our price as follows:

	Universal $
94,000 tons mixed nuts	71,000
1,400,000 tons brown sugar	9,000
9,000,000,000,000,000 gallons soured cream	111,000
82,000 tons dried carrots (organically grown)	30,000
1,800,000 tons garlic	11,000
1 egg	319,000
Subtotal	551,000

Materials	551,000
Labour	44,900
VAT	449,000
Service	130,000
Sub (sub) total	44,900
Cover charge	47,390
Subtotal	1,267,190
TOTAL (+ VAT and including materials)	2,983,380

**MURPHY AND MURPHY
LTD
Formerly
Murphy and
Murphy**

Dear Sirs

Re Your Advertisement

Please see our price below. We trust that it meets your requirements.

97,000,000,000,000,000,000,000,000,000 tons of peat	37 dollars
Delivery of above	9,724,134,600 dollars
TOTAL	9,724,134,637 dollars

Please find enclosed our estimate for your recently
advertised project.

Universal Dollars

Polyfilla	94,000	"
Tetrion All-purpose Filler	82,000	"
Plastic wood	71,000	"
Creosote	11,000	"
Rubber bands	87,000	"
Evostick	50,000	"
Ronstrip	111,000	"
6 in. nails	32,000	"
Elastic bands	1	"
Gravel	0.90	"
Labour	0.21	"
Sub total	538,002.11	
VAT @ 15%	80,700.32	
	618,702.43 Universal Dollars	

Fforbes Browne
HIGH CLASS ARTEFACTS FOR THE GENTRY

Herewith our considered estimate for the work required.

46,000,000,000,000,000 million square miles Axminster carpets	99 million guineas
25,000 solid gold trees and assorted vegetation	38 million guineas
94 million rolls Sanderson (Limestone scenery) wallpaper	47 million guineas
6 variable-flow electric waterfalls	3 million guineas
Fur coat and jewellery (for woman)	1 million guineas
Jaguar XJS (for man)	2 million guineas
	190 million guineas
TOTAL tip	10 million guineas
	200 million guineas

---

super-trans-intercontinental inc.
(BUILDERS & MEGALOMANIACS)

QUOTATION

Our finest price for your projected work-situation is enclosed for your reference.

1 Freeway system	96,000 dollars
12 major cities or urban areas	143,000,000 dollars
1 President (or cash equivalent)	3 dollars
1 major chain of mountains thrown up to a height of over 12,000 feet in certain areas	2,741,000,001 dollars
6 assorted Walt Disney characters	36 dollars
14 Statues of Liberty	33,000 dollars
1 Capitalist economy based on a free-market economy and universal suffrage	2 dollars
TOTAL	2,884,129,042 dollars

Global Worlds Pty

Estimate

Re: New World

Please find below our price for your tender

	Universal $
Labour	250,000
Parts/Materials (ex-factory)	97,000
Cement	151,000
Net	498,000
VAT	59,760
TOTAL	557,760
MISCELLANEOUS	1,500,000
GRAND TOTAL	2,057,760

(10% reduction for cash settlement)

The Amazing Marco

Conjuring Artiste
Extraordinaire

ONE WORLD

In accordance with the instructions issued
by your company, I am attaching the terms
of a 1 (one) evening performance in which to
conjure up the required article.

```
                               94 dollars
                                6 dollars
LABOUR                    250,000 dollars
ASSISTANT'S LABOUR
INSURANCE

           TOTAL   250,100 dollars
```

(Rabbits, doves, etc. extra)

---

goldberg's
"To you, my son"

OUR QUOTATION

Enclosed for you our estimate for preparing a high quality, de
luxe world. If we can be of help, ring us and without delay we
will be round.

```
    1 kosher firmament              45,000,000 shekels
    1 kosher selection of beasts
    that creepeth                    2,000,000    " .
    1 kosher whale                          48    "
    selection of finest kosher grass
    and herb yielding seed               3,100    "
    97,000,000 synagogues           96,000,000    "
    1 man (of the faith)         2,000,000,000,000 "
    1 woman (also of the faith) 2,000,000,000,000  "
                        TOTAL   4,000,143,003,148 shekels
```

```
234987 AMALWORLDS G
112 GOD G
001/AB

ATTN: T.G. COHEN-COHEN

HORRIFIED TO LEARN THAT BOARD IS STARTING TO MUTTER ABOUT
CANCELLATION OF PROJECT.  PLEASED  TO INFORM THAT ONLY TODAY
RECEIVED BROCHURE FROM FIRM BUILDERS OFFERING CHEAP CHEAP
CREATIONS.  4 TO 6 DAYS MAXIMUM.  AM MOSTLY IMPRESSED.
SHOULD IMAGINE THIS MIGHT BE BIG BREAKFAST = SORRY, BIG
BREAK = WE HAVE BEEN WAITING FOR.  AM SENDING COPY BROCHURE
UNDER SEPARATE COVER FOR YOUR INSPECTION.  WILL INVESTIGATE
FURTHER.  PLEASE CONFIRM PROJECT NOT YET CANCELLED.  MEET
ME UNDER CLOCK TONIGHT.  BIG BABS.

GOD


112 GOD G
234987 AMALWORLDS G
```

With the compliments of

RAY SCRUMMAGE
Director

COSMIC & UNIVERSAL CONSTRUCTION
General Builders & Contra

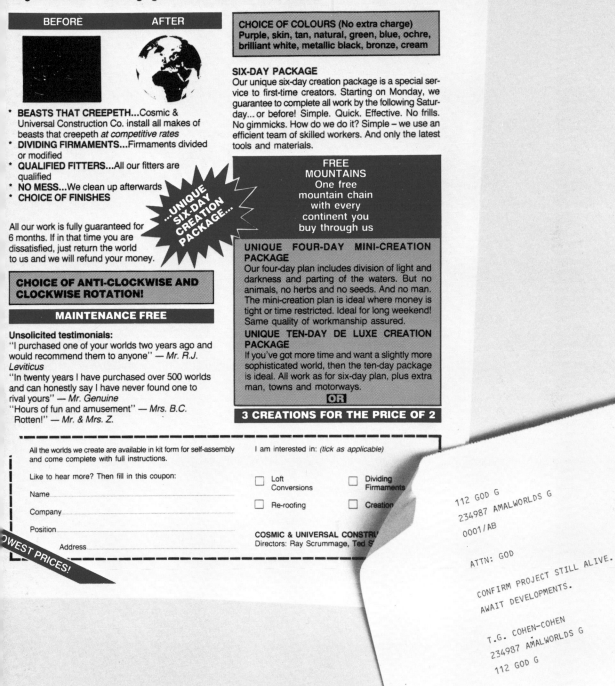

COSMIC & UNIVERSAL CONSTRUCTION CO.

General Builders & Contractors

3rd Arch Along
Limepit Viaduct
Telephone 18194804612 (one line)
Telex CONU

MEMBER OF THE FEDERATION OF SMALL BUILDERS
AND BUILDING CONTRACTORS

Dear God,

Re: Creation of World

Thank you for your enquiry. Of course we would be delighted to quote
for building you a world. Perhaps, though, I should point out at this
juncture that we ourselves haven't actually as yet built a complete world,
though we have seen lots of pictures and read lots of books about it.
However, I feel sure that, given our considerable experience of damp coursing
and loft conversion, together with a touch of luck, we shall have no problem
in meeting your every need.

Of course you ought to realise that all building work is much the same.
And that just because a firm hasn't perhaps the experience of a more established outfit, it isn't any drawback. Take fountains for example. A year
ago we hadn't built a single ornamental fountain. Not one. Yet this year
we've done nearly two. And all of them are working properly. Even the one
where the water comes out of the dolphin's mouth.

And take loft extensions. We must have done dozens of them by now -
well, nine at any rate. Yet five years ago, if you'd come to me and said
'Show me what you've done with dormer windows', I'd have had to say 'Not a
bloody thing, mate'. And thirty years ago, before I was born, well, I'd
never have imagined the many ways you can add an extra room to your house.
Which just goes to show.

It's like riding a bike. Or sex. I mean, you never know till you've
tried, do you? But once you've tried you never forget. And you never fall
off again either. At least that goes for riding a bike.

And how many world-famous novelists would have known they could write
a major new blockbusting bestseller if they didn't start at some point? If
they didn't think, 'By golly, I'll give it a crack'? Blimey, I bet loads
and loads of people said to them beforehand, 'You can't write, you're only
a -----------' (whatever their job was). Yet pretty soon they'd be jolly
well forced to say, 'Crikey, you can write after all'.

And the same goes for us. Not that we can teach you how to ride a
bike, or become a bestselling author. Or even how to make love. Though
we can probably recommend someone who can help you if that's what you're
after. But we can help you with your creation.

What's more, we'll give you a free quote first. And we don't overcharge.

Yours enthusiastically,

Ray Scrummage
Ray Scrummage
For Cosmic & Universal Construction Co.

"god"

CREATIVE CONSULTANCY PROPERTY SERVICING
Agent for: AMALGAMATED WORLDS Pty.

Registered Office: UNIT 4, LEVEL 2, CENTRAL PLAZA
Telephone: 353 500000 Telex: GOD
Directors: GOD (Managing, Sales, Financial)

Dear Mr. Cohen-Cohen,

Re: Creation of The World

I have just received a reply from the Cosmic & Universal
Construction Company. I have looked through the dictionary
twice now and still can't quite find a word to describe
my reaction. Somewhere between shock and dismay is close,
though I think perhaps 'abject horror' sums it up best.

It would appear that they've never actually built a world,
and that the nearest they have come to it is, in fact, a
set of ornamental fountains with a dolphin in the middle.
They've never written a letter either from the looks of it.
At least not one with decent grammar.

However - and this is a big however - they _are_ keen. _And_
they're very cheap. Which is in their favour.

What should we do? Do we pursue the matter? I'm at a loss
to decide.

Yours concernedly,

Veronica Makepiece

PP. God

Dear God,

Re: Creation Of World

I've just read your letter and appreciate your reaction.
While one applauds initiative and enthusiasm, one needs
to temper it with a little realism.

I'm sure Cosmic & Universal Construction mean well - these
firms always do. But creating a completely new world is no
doddle; it is a tricky business. Very tricky. And I must
advise that the builders be informed of this before they
fully commit themselves to any work.

In view of this, I find myself torn between a strong desire
to say 'No', and an equally strong desire to say 'Hang it all,
yes'. After much heart-searching I have at last decided to
ask you to request that the builders supply us with their
fullest estimate and schedule. Only this way can we realisti-
cally assess whether the involvement of this firm is a viable
proposition. And please, do stress the importance of the
work at hand. We cannot, I'm afraid, afford mistakes.

Yours cautiously,

T.G. Cohen-Cohen

T.G. Cohen-Cohen
Project Development Officer

AMALGAMATED WORLDS Pty

BIGGEST IN THE UNIVERSE

AMALGAMATED WORLDS PTY
AMALGAMATED WORLDS CORPORATION HOUSE
AMALGAMATED WORLDS CORPORATION PLAZA
AMALGAMATED WORLDS CORPORATION AVENUE
AMALGAMATED WORLDS CORPORATION VILLE

TELEPHONE: 964359214 to 954359792 (inclusive)
TELEX: AMALWORLDS

Dear God,

Re: Creation of World

Thinking this afternoon about my decision to stop Cosmic &
Universal Construction, I was suddenly struck by the absurdity
of my last letter. Of course the project is important. Of
course we can't afford to lose. Of course Cosmic & Universal
Construction must be made aware of the importance of the work
at hand. But we are at this stage only talking of estimates
and possibilities. There is after all no obligation on the
part of either party.

At the risk of changing with the wind, for which I beg your
pardon, might I beg you to speak to your man at the company,
asking him to quote. Make sure there are no promises. And
that you put nothing in writing. I'm sure I can rely on you
to come up with a satisfactory excuse. (Have we used the
plague-of-wombats one yet?).

Yours sincerely,

Tracey Goldberg

G. Cohen-Cohen
Project Development Officer

AMALGAMATED WORLDS Pty

BIGGEST IN THE UNIVERSE

AMALGAMATED WORLDS PTY
AMALGAMATED WORLDS CORPORATION HOUSE
AMALGAMATED WORLDS CORPORATION PLAZA
AMALGAMATED WORLDS CORPORATION AVENUE
AMALGAMATED WORLDS CORPORATION VILLE

TELEPHONE: 964359214 to 954359792 (inclusive)
TELEX: AMALWORLDS

Dear God,

Re: Creation Of World

On second thoughts, I don't know that it would be quite such
a good idea for Cosmic & Universal Construction to do the
work. Enthusiasm and zeal are all very well, but together
they are no substitute for experience. I hate to pour cold
water on the whole thing but, after a sleepless night considering the project, I fear it would not be at all prudent for
Cosmic & Universal Construction to waste their/your/my/
everyone's time.

I would therefore beg you ask them not to involve themselves
any further. Perhaps you could think up a suitable excuse.
I know you are very good at this sort of thing, having had a
lifetime's experience of it.

Yours regretfully,

Tracey Goldberg

pp T.G. Cohen-Cohen
Project Development Officer

Dear Mr. Cohen-Cohen,

Re: Creation Of The World

As requested, I have been in touch again with my man at
Cosmic & Universal Construction. The indecision on our
part seemed to dampen his enthusiasm not one whit, and he
is on the phone constantly to talk about the project. All
this week he has been bombarding me with designs for the
new world, and I do warn you that some are a trifle eccentric
(to say the least). I've asked him to polish them up a bit
before I pass them on to you.

On a more cheerful note, I have at long last discovered a
company that offers good, reasonably-priced insurance deals.
And while I'm sure cost is not everything with a project of
this importance, it is at least comforting to know we may
be able to make a small saving on our budget.

With best wishes,

Veronica Makepi...

PP. God

IVOR GOLDFILLING & V.V. R...
INSURANCE BROKERS

Dear Mr. God,

   Further to our meeting last week at which you
expressed a wish to arrange insurance through our
office, I now have pleasure in supplying you with
the policy document for such cover. Would you
please be so kind as to examine this thoroughly
and contact me should there be any points you are
not sure on. Otherwise I will assume you are
satisfied with the terms of the policy and will
go ahead and complete all necessary arrangements.
With this in mind, I would anticipate you being
able to assume complete insurance cover by the
end of next week at the latest.

                    y...

        Ivor...

BODDLERS ASSURANCE COMPANY LIMITED

The Company agrees with the policyholder to provide insurance as
expressed in this policy during any period of insurance in respect
of which the policyholder has paid, or agreed to pay, the premium
(see very boring notes at rear of document).

Definition of The World
For the purposes of the insurance the expression 'World' used herein
shall mean a large round blob described in 1 (a) Descriptions of Blobs
in the 'Certification of World Insurances' (hereinafter referred to in
this Policy as 'The Certificate') being the number of this policy as
the Certificate Number and which, having been delivered to the
Policyholder, remains effective (the rest of this paragraph has been
deleted due to lack of space). (And interest.)

THE POLICYHOLDER'S ATTENTION IS PARTICULARLY DRAWN TO CONDITION
9/64/567/A(b)/23/az (357862) OF THIS POLICY

Insurance Provided

1. Where the Insurance Provided is comprehensive, all clauses of
this policy are applicable.

2. Where the Insurance Provided is 'third party, fire and theft'
only, Clauses III, IV, V and VII of this policy are not applicable,
and Clauses I and XXXII apply only in respect of loss or damage to
the world caused directly by fire, self-ignition, lightning, explosion,
theft, or attempted theft. In addition, Clause XX applies only in
respect of damage caused by theft, fire, flood, locusts, combustible
stolen locusts, enormous plagues of pigeons and plagues of herrings.
Clause VIII applies only in respect of plagues of haddocks and
exploding blacmanges. Clause XVI doesn't apply unless you're a haddock.
Clause IX applies on Mondays and alternate Tuesdays. Clause X doesn't
apply (unless previously applied for).

3. Where the Insurance Provided is 'third party' only, Clauses I, III,
IV, V and VI and Condition 7 of this policy are not applicable except on
Saturdays, wet Wednesdays and Monday to Thursday (April to mid-October)
inclusive. And it serves you right for being so tight with your money.

Loss of or damage to The World
Clause I
The Company will pay for the loss of or damage to the World (including
its accessories and spare parts or components. But not including spare
accessories or spare components. Except spare components with no spare
accessories.) Payment may be made at the Company's option either for
the full cost of repair, reinstatement or replacement, or by cash for
the amount of the loss or damage agreed between the Company and the
Policyholder, but not in any event exceeding the reasonable market value
at the time of the loss or damage (the rest of this paragraph has been
deleted due to lack of sense).

Towing Charges
The Company will also pay the reasonable cost of protection and removal
to the nearest repairers, if as a result of any loss or damage insured under
this Clause the world is disabled.

Page 2

The Company will not pay for:

a. Depreciation, wear and tear, mechanical or electrical breakdown, or anything else whatsoever.

b. Anything else at all not covered in (a.) above.

c. Damage by frost.

d. Damage by overeating.

e. Damage by vandals who smash up phone booths, leaving them with ripped up directories, filthy graffiti written all over the very code you need to see, and as for the smell....It'd be all the same if it was their own mother lying half-dead in the gutter while they searched for a booth that was in working order, wouldn't it? And as for (the rest of this paragraph has been deleted due to hysteria).

Clause II

There is no Clause II.

Clause III

See Clause II.

The
Insured
Person

Clause VII

For the purposes of insurance under this condition the term 'Insured Person' (as distinct from 'Insured Haddock') shall mean any one or more of the following:

a. The Policyholder.

b. Any person using the World with the permission of the Policyholder for social, domestic and pleasure purposes, where such use is permitted by the terms of this Certificate.

c. See (a.) above.

d. Not applicable.

Clause IX

The Company will pay for any loss of, or damage to, rugs, clothing and personal effects occurring in or on the World by fire, theft, attempted fire, attempted theft, or attempted sexual intercourse.

The Company will not pay for loss of or damage to:

a. Money, stamps, documents or securities.

b. Goods or samples carried in connection with any trade.

Page 3

Clause IX
(cont.)

c. Anything else.

d. This piece of paper.

e. Any other piece of paper.

f. Any goods or dead haddock carried in connection with any trade.

g. See press for details.

Clause XIXIIIVIX

Cancelled due to lack of numerical ability.

GENERAL EXCEPTIONS

The Company will not pay for:

a. Accident, injury or damage occurring during the period Monday to Sunday (inclusive).

b. Any accident, injury, loss or damage occurring if to the knowledge of the Policyholder the World is being used, spun, or otherwise gyrated in a wild, dangerous, or reckless manner.

c. Any liability which attaches by virtue of an agreement but which would not have attached in the absence of such agreement (for further details see solicitor attached to rear of this document).

"god"

CREATIVE CONSULTANCY PROPERTY SERVICING
Agent for: AMALGAMATED WORLDS Pty.
Registered Office: UNIT 4, LEVEL 2, CENTRAL PLAZA
Telephone: 353 500000 Telex: GOD
Directors: GOD (Managing, Sales, Financial)

Dear Mr. Cohen-Cohen,

Re: Creation of World

I am enclosing herewith the first proposals from Cosmic &
Universal Construction. I'm not sure they are quite what
we envisaged. In fact, I'm fairly sure they're not. I should
also point out that the lurid lime green Pentel of the
original copy has not reproduced particularly well.

Trusting that you are now fully recovered from your attack
of shingles.

Yours faithfully,

Veronica Makepiece

PP. God

Enclosures

COSMIC & UNIVERSAL CONSTRUCTION CO.
General Builders & Contractors
3rd Arch Along
Limepit Viaduct
Telephone 18194804612 (one line)
Telex CONU

MEMBER OF THE FEDERATION OF SMALL BUILDERS
AND BUILDING CONTRACTORS

Dear Mr. God,

Thank you for your letter. We quite understand the obligation
which you stress in your 11-page letter and 3-page synopsis (with
1½ pages of footnotes). And we fully appreciate the importance of
this project which is described so comprehensively in the 36-page
letter from your solicitor.

With due regard to all that was said therein, we now supply
herewith our rough designs and estimates. Plus our suggested
'Six-Day Plan'.

We trust that these will meet with your approval.

Yours faithfully,

Gwyn MacTaggart (Secretary)

Gwyn MacTaggart
Dictated by Mr. Scrummage
and signed in his absence

A FEW IDEAS:-

MAN

NAUGHTY BIT

optional bit

DRY BITS

WET BITS

COSTS

Bricks $25
Cement $11
Rubber Mastic $10
2" Copper Pipe $6
New Zealand (self assembly) $21
Africa (taps not inc.) $43
6 x Volcanoes (seconds) $38
ONE Canada (slightly damaged) 30 cents
ONE Australia (shop soiled) $40
Miscellaneous $10
Glue $16
ONE Man $40

TOTAL: $254.30
less discount: $200.00
                $54.30

B-SCREW

SCREW

VERY LARGE SCREW

MOUNTAIN

METHOD OF FIXING MOUNTAIN TO CEILING (AUSTRALIA ONLY)

NAUGHTY BITS

RIGGED BITS VERY VERY LARGE SCREW INDEED

METHOD OF FIXING MOUNTAIN TO GROUND

LARGE SCREW

METHOD OF FIXING TREE TO GROUND

① LARGE SCREW
Method of fixing man's head to shoulders.

② GLUE NAIL
Alternative method of sticking man's head to shoulders.
CEMENT
STICKING PLASTER
WALLPAPER PASTE

SIX-DAY PLAN

Day One   Morning Arrive - put up portable toilet/put up
           portable offices/put up portable workshop/put up
           portable billiards room/erect scaffolding

           Afternoon Half day's rest from labours

Day Two   Day of rest

Day Three Morning Divide light and darkness/divide land
           and water/gather waters/gather herbs/gather seeds/
           gather grass/gather fruit

           Afternoon Half day's rest from all that dividing
           and gathering

Day Four   Fix plumbing

Day Five   Day of rest .

Day Six   Morning Make day/make night/bring forth moving
           creatures/and birds/and living creatures that moveth/
           assemble man

           Afternoon Take down portable toilet/take down port-
           able offices/take down portable workshop/take down
           scaffolding/clean up site

CREATIVE CONSULTANCY PROPERTY SERVICING
Agent for: AMALGAMATED WORLDS Pty.
Registered Office: UNIT 4, LEVEL 2, CENTRAL PLAZA
Telephone: 353 500000 Telex: GOD
Directors: GOD (Managing, Sales, Financial)

Dear Mr. Cohen-Cohen,

Re: Creation of The World

Last time I wrote to you, you will recall I was a little
worried by the direction in which the proposals from the
Cosmic & Universal Construction Company appeared to be
moving.

I am afraid these proposals have now become cause for
further alarm. I wrote to Mr. Scrummage, the man handling
the work for Cosmic & Universal Construction, pointing out
that the extensive use of wood and nails, while structurally
sound, was not likely to appeal to the aesthetic eye, and
requesting they incorporate more flair into their designs.

It was with some surprise, therefore, that I received a
somewhat curt reply pointing out that flair costs money
and that they personally couldn't see anything wrong with
the designs.

I suggested they might supply us with another batch of
proposals, which duly arrived on my desk this morning. I
regret that they only served to confirm my worst fears. I
have drafted a long letter to Mr. Scrummage to try and
clear matters up. Here, for your reference, are the proposals
as laid out by the Cosmic & Universal Construction Company.

On a more favourable note, I have discovered a company that
constructs off-the-peg men. The results seem promising and
I have arranged a meeting with a representative from the
company to discuss the matter. Enclosed herewith for your
reference only is the company's brochure.

Yours as ever,

Veronica Makepiece

pp. God

Enclosures

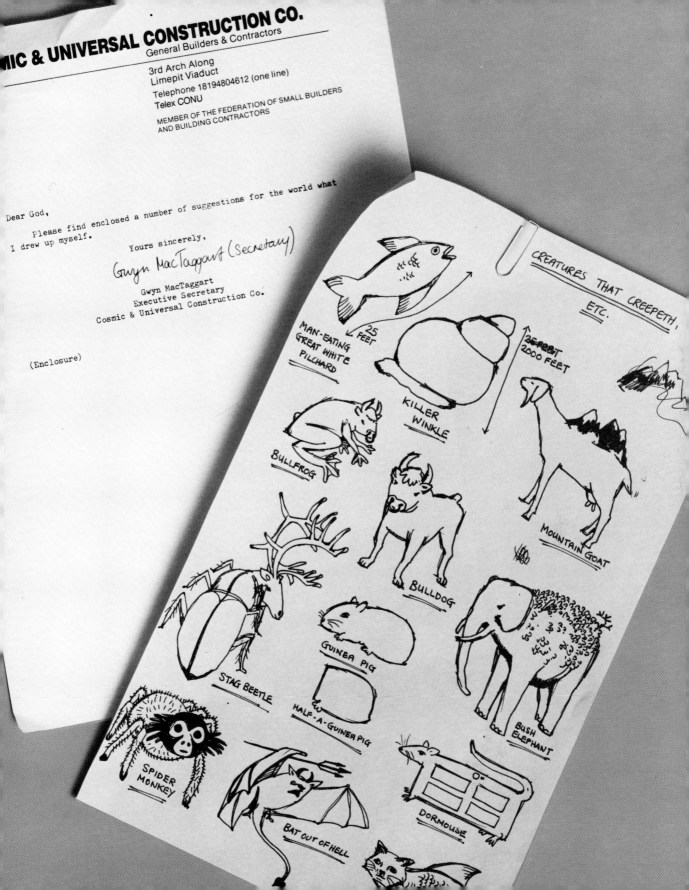

MIC & UNIVERSAL CONSTRUCTION CO.
General Builders & Contractors

3rd Arch Along
Limepit Viaduct
Telephone 18194804612 (one line)
Telex CONU

MEMBER OF THE FEDERATION OF SMALL BUILDERS
AND BUILDING CONTRACTORS

Dear God,

    Please find enclosed a number of suggestions for the world what
I drew up myself.

                Yours sincerely,

                Gwyn MacTaggart (Secretary)

                Gwyn MacTaggart
                Executive Secretary
      Cosmic & Universal Construction Co.

(Enclosure)

GRAVE-AN-IMAGE LTD

A member of the Widenberger Group of Companies

Imagine the scene. A new creation. A brand new world. It should be an enjoyable time; a time filled with happiness and thanksgiving. Yet all too often it's a time of sadness and regret. Why? Because not enough time has gone into the choice of the man to live in that world. Of course no one can be sure they've constructed exactly the right sort of man. But we like to think we've come as close as possible to *eliminating all avoidable error*, by listing all details of man on our computer. That means you get the man you want. Or something very close to it. Because we match your requirements to the men available.

With GRAVE-AN-IMAGE we guarantee to supply you with a suitable man for the job, or your money back. Just fill in the simple questionnaire below. And we'll supply you with a sample man by return.

- -

JUST TICK THE ONE WHO MOST
NEARLY MATCHES YOUR
REQUIREMENTS

I would like the man to be:
- ☐ liken to me (please enclose photo)
- ☐ liken to someone else (please enclose someone else's photo)
- ☐ liken to Donny Osmond (please don't enclose photo)
- ☐ liken to Howard Hughes (please enclose wallet)
- ☐ liken to Randolph Hearst (please enclose lawyer)

His hair must be:
- ☐ black
- ☐ brown
- ☐ grey
- ☐ green
- ☐ machine-washable

His skin must be:
- ☐ wrinkled
- ☐ grey
- ☐ tanned
- ☐ machine-washable

His hobbies must be:
- ☐ football
- ☐ duckshooting
- ☐ macramé and embroidery
- ☐ speedway and other butch pursuits
- ☐ Spanish Military History 1680-1750

I would like his temperament to be:
- ☐ cool
- ☐ hot
- ☐ medium
- ☐ medium dry

I would like him to have:
- ☐ 1 leg
- ☐ 3 legs
- ☐ 17 legs

To GRAVE-AN-IMAGE LIMITED

Yes, I am interested in your services. Please rush me absolutely everything you've got on the subject even if it means you have to get up from your desk and open a drawer in your filing cabinet.

Name .... (please state alternative age) ....

Age ....

Address ....

Where you hide your back door key ....

AMALGAMATED WORLDS Pty

BIGGEST IN THE UNIVERSE

· AMALGAMATED WORLDS PTY
AMALGAMATED WORLDS CORPORATION HOUSE
AMALGAMATED WORLDS CORPORATION PLAZA
AMALGAMATED WORLDS CORPORATION AVENUE
AMALGAMATED WORLDS CORPORATION VILLE

TELEPHONE: 964359214 to 954359792 (inclusive)
TELEX: AMALWORLDS

Dear God,

Re: Creation of World

At last some reasonable news! After much persuasion on my part,
the Board of Directors of Amalgamated Worlds have agreed to
issue a provisional contract for the Creation of the World.

I should point out that the Directors were not a little sceptical
about the whole project. In fact, to be brutally frank, they
were downright cynical. Very downright cynical. (That was the
reaction of the more generous ones; the rest simply scoffed and
refused even to discuss the matter.)

Nevertheless, they did agree and this I consider to be quite an
achievement under the circumstances. However, it was only
brought about after much bending of the ear, and no less bending
of the arm. I mention this because I fear that in the cold light
of day there will be a good deal of recrimination and reconsideration.

The end result is that, in persuading the Board to go ahead with
the Creation I have put myself in a pretty unenviable position.
I must ask you to stress again to the builders that the work
must be finished on time! And to budget!! If they don't come up
with the goods, I'm for the high jump - which at Amalgamated
Worlds has a habit of being very high indeed. I don't need to
remind you that your own predicament wouldn't be too enviable
either if they fail to do their stuff on time and within budget.

Perhaps when you write to the builders you could ask them to return
the attached contract as soon as possible. All they need to do
is sign on the dotted line. That is assuming they can write.

Yours as ever,

T.G. Cohen-Cohen

T.G. Cohen-Cohen
Project Development Officer

Enclosure

REMEMBER
NO SMELLS

Dear Mr. Scrummage,

Re: Creation Of World

I have received from Mr. Cohen-Cohen the draft contract for
the above project which I think you will find pretty comprehensive.
As you will see, I have underlined a few items. I should point
out that you are to indemnify us against any claims that arise
out of your negligence, and that you must be prepared to offer
full guarantees for all work undertaken.

I think you ought to realise that signing a legal document does
in fact involve you in contractual obligation, and that failure
to meet that contractual obligation could involve you in expensive
litigation. I point this out only because I know you're not
altogether familiar with work of this nature and I would not wish
you to enter into a legally binding contract without being fully
aware of the implications of doing so. I should in passing point
out that our clients - Amalgamated Worlds - were most insistent
that the World be completed on time! To budget! Or else!

Usually bully-boy tactics don't wash with me. But in this case
the bully is very big. So, in this case, I suggest it might be
wise to fulfil their every request.

Perhaps you could sign the contract and return it to me. Please
don't hesitate to phone sho... ...y problems.

Yours respectfully,

Veronica Ma...

PP. God

THIS IS
V.V.V.
IMPORTANT

Enclosure

A Contract

* WRITE YOUR COMPANY'S NAME HERE

This contract is hereby issued on the ....
day of .... between *................................
.... and .... for the Creation (hereinafter
referred to as 'The Creation') of (hereinafter referred to as 'of')
the World (hereinafter referred to as 'The World').

This contract shall refer and afford unto the said hereinafter persons
all deed and trust as hereinbefore so ferred to. Terms as hereinso-
before listed.

PLEASE NOTE ||

The World shall comprise one large round object being of sound
construction and design that shall revolve in a revolvewise direction.
This object shall be capable of spinning in an orbit around other
objects, and shall be so constructed so that bits don't keep falling off and annoying people. Even persons who jolly well deserved
to be annoyed. And any bits which do fall off, excepting those
which are purposely designed to do so, shall be replaced immediately.
If not before.

PLEASE ENSURE || NO CORNERS

The World shall comprise only bits which are large or round. The
World shall not comprise bits which are square or pointed or which
have nasty sharp corners or dangerous sharp edges (other than a
few bits which can be sharp and dangerous on purpose).

The World shall be of a subdued colour, being definitely not pink.
Or lime green. And it shall not be covered in a nasty pseudo-
flock wallpaper. Or those cork floor tiles that come up at the
corners and catch your toe when you get up in the middle of the
night for a glass of water. Or nasty brick-effect stick-on plastic
sheeting. Or horrible floral motif ceiling tiles that you can't
get off even with hot water and a sharp scraper.

World shall not make a grinding sound when it goes round.
 horrible tinny sound that sets your teeth on edge. And
ustn't smell either. The World shall not smell of burning
tic or burning floral motif ceiling tiles.   And that goes
 smoke too. It mustn't give out belching clouds of black
 e whenever it goes round.

onstruction of the aforementioned World hereinbefore referred
nd hereinafter referred to, all work shall use specified
rials. In particular no 'dodgy' materials shall be used,
 if they're very cheap. Nor shall any 'no-questions-asked'
rials be used (such terms to include those materials which
le 'don't want to talk about, John (know what I mean)').

World shall be built in a period not exceeding 7 (seven) days,
uding 1 (one) day's rest. If the period not exceeding 7
en) days shall exceed 7 (seven) days, then a penalty clause
einafter referred to as 'The Penalty Clause') shall be invoked
h shall hereafter bring so to bear such penalties as be
eed fit by those who shall be required to determine such
lties. In particular, all penalties will be judged by a
l of judges (hereinafter referred to as 'The Judgement Panel')
shall be so required to judge all penalties.

he event of the full 7 (seven) days not being required to
lete the work, then all those days not required will not
required.

 All time required to complete such work as shall be
 completed shall be recorded in a book which shall be
 of reasonable quality so people don't say 'Crumbs,
 they can't be much of a firm if they can only afford a
 book like this'. All details of time taken to do
 each job shall be recorded in this book, which shall
 be made fully available to any person wishing to
 inspect such records. Where such records are not
 required to be so inspected, then it shall not be

---

1) Continued

necessary for a record to be produced. However, if
someone changes their mind and says, 'I think I'd
rather like to see those records after all', then
they shall be allowed so to do.

2)
Whereinsobefore and hereunto The World is completed,
a deed stating that The World is complete shall be
presented to any person or persons wishing to see
such deed.

Notes

1.
The notes which hereinafter follow shall be referred
to as 'The Notes'.

2.
No other notes shall be allowed to be called 'The Notes'
in order to avoid confusion.
No other part of this document shall be referred to as
'The Notes'.
The word Notes will have plenty of space around it so
you don't have to keep looking through the whole document
trying to find it.
A special pamphlet entitled 'Where To Find The Notes'
shall be published and supplied as an appendix to
this document.
Persons will be encouraged to look for The Notes by lots
of handy hints at the bottom of other pages saying things
like 'This way to The Notes' and 'Notes coming soon' and
'I bet you can't wait till we come to the bit about The
Notes'.

7.
There are no more Notes after this one.

8.
Except this one.

9.
This is the very, very last Note.

This document is witnessed and sealed on the .... day of
....
between ....
.... and ....
....
(Witness)
....

"God"

CREATIVE CONSULTANCY PROPERTY SERVICING
Agent for: AMALGAMATED WORLDS Pty.

Registered Office: UNIT 4, LEVEL 2, CENTRAL PLAZA
Telephone: 353 500000 Telex: GOD
Directors: GOD (Managing, Sales, Financial)

Dear Mr. Scrummage,

Re: Creation Of The World

Thank you for returning the contract and for your most
unusual letter. May I first of all say that the idea of
anything remotely untoward, as you intimate in your letter,
is quite out of the question. No amount of financial
inducement - even 50 per cent or more (and I must say 50
per cent is a remarkably good reduction) - will persuade
me to break the law. And I hope this warning against
mischievous practices will be borne in mind when entering
into any other agreements with me in the future. It would
look pretty squalid if this new world, from which so much
prestige can be gained, were to become burdened by even
the slightest hint of corruption.

I have now returned the contract to Amalgamated Worlds.
After due consideration I have decided not to offer any
explanation of the stains to them. They tend to be humour-
less people and might well fail to be amused. I feel we
should let them puzzle the cause and nature of the stains
themselves and come to whatever conclusions they may choose.

rs sincerely,

nica Makepiece

MIC & UNIVERSAL CONSTRUCTION CO.
General Builders & Contractors

3rd Arch Along
Limepit Viaduct
Telephone 18194804612 (one line)
Telex CONU

MEMBER OF THE FEDERATION OF SMALL BUILDERS
AND BUILDING CONTRACTORS

Re: Creation of World

Dear God,

As requested, we are returning the contract to you, duly signed and
dated. Please excuse the rather sticky stain on the second page which I
assure you is only coffee, even if it doesn't look like that. And the
suspicious-looking marks on the third page are nothing more than wood
preserver.

I wonder if I might take this opportunity to draw your attention to
one other matter: namely, the advantages of 'cash only' payments to both
builder and customer. As you may already know, we in the building trade
pay our way just like the next man. And when it comes to taxes, we are
every bit as conscientious as the average wage-earner, if not more so.
I don't want you to get the impression that we're trying to dodge things
or do anything that isn't 100 per cent straight down the line, but I think
you should be told when there's a chance to save a bit of brass. Not that
I'm suggesting anything, you understand. The decision is entirely yours. But
if you were to pay cash - and don't get me wrong, no one's suggesting you
should - then you could save yourself a tidy sum. In fact, about 50 per
cent. That is if you're interested.

If you're not, then that's fine by me. If you want to spend 100 or
even 200 per cent more than you have to, that's your business. I mean,
it's entirely up to you if you want to fork out a small fortune just
because you think it's morally wrong to pull a swanker, even when every
other Tom, Dick and Harry is on the fiddle left, right and centre.

Don't let me influence you in any way. But if you do happen to want
to make a saving, then the offer's there. If you know what I mean.

Yours cordially,

Ray Scrummage

Ray Scrummage
For Cosmic & Universal Construction Co.

AMALGAMATED WORLDS Pty
BIGGEST IN THE UNIVERSE

AMALGAMATED WORLDS PTY
AMALGAMATED WORLDS CORPORATION HOUSE
AMALGAMATED WORLDS CORPORATION PLAZA
AMALGAMATED WORLDS CORPORATION AVENUE
AMALGAMATED WORLDS CORPORATION VILLE

TELEPHONE: 964359214 to 954359792 (inclusive)
TELEX: AMALWORLDS

Dear Sir(s),

CREATION OF THE WORLD

My underling, T.G. Cohen-Cohen, has suggested that I
might drop you a line in my capacity as Managing
Director of Amalgamated Worlds to tell you how
pleased we are that the above project has got off
the ground (although it's about time). It is with
very great pleasure that I can now allow you to
thank me for permitting you to embark upon this
project.

It is a project that I trust you will carry out to
the best of your abilities and which my staff and
I will be glad to help you with in any way possible.

I hope that you will enjoy working with Amalgamated
Worlds ~~and I look forward to seeing you when you
are next in the area.~~

With my best wishes,

R.V. Goldenstein

R.V. Goldenstein (Mrs)
Managing Director

CREATIVE CONSULTANCY PROPERTY SERVIC[...]
Agent for: AMALGAMATED WORLDS Pty.
Registered Office: UNIT 4, LEVEL 2, CENTRAL PLAZA[...]
Telephone: 353 500000 Telex: GOD
Directors: GOD (Managing, Sales, Financial)

Dear Mr. Cohen-Cohen,

Re: Creation Of The World

Thank you for all your recent letters. Please tell Mrs Goldenstein that I am equally pleased that the project is now under way.

I continue to receive letters of advice from many authorities which I believe may be of interest. When you have had a chance to study them, perhaps you would return them to me, together with any comments.

Yours sincerely,

Veronica Makepiece

Contagious Disea[...]

INCORPORATING UNITED COUGHS, CONSOLIDATED WHEEZES AND UNIVERSAL ILLNESS

Dear God,

Thank you for your letter requesting our prices for supplying assorted diseases.

However, we very much regret that, following an unfortunate incident involving a fragile test tube, a highly contagious substance and a solid stone floor, the staff here have fallen victim to a particularly virulent attack of pestilence, and are at present unable to offer any help.

However, if you are willing to call round to our offices and stand by an open window, then I feel sure we could supply you with any diseases you might require.

Yours contagiously,

Stanley Goodwin

Stanley Goodwin
Sales Department

---

rainy/days

SUPPLIERS OF CLIMATE, WEATHER AND ASSORTED METEOROLOGY

My dear God,

Re: Creation of The World

Please find enclosed a sample of the climates we now have in stock. We would confirm our prices as follows:

Polar Climate — Includes ice, snow, wind, rain, sleet, plus 240-page operating manual

$155.00

Temperate Climate — Includes ice, snow, wind, rain, sleet, and one day of sunshine

$225.00

Tropical Climate — Includes sun, sun, and isolated showers (optional extras include monsoon, typhoons, hurricanes and snow)

$330.00

Equatorial Climate — Includes sun, sun, and sun (optional extras include sunglasses)

$960.00

Yours sincerely,

Seamus MacIntosh.

Seamus MacIntosh
For Rainy Days

MARSH LANDS

EVERYTHING FOR YOUR BOG

Dear God,

Thank you for your letter inquiring after our 'Marsh Hire' service. We supply a number of different marshes and swamps both for hire and rental and feel sure you will find something to suit your needs. Our standard range consists of:

Junior Swamp 4' x 6' with clip-on fixing. Can be rolled up and put away when not required.

Economy Swamp A tough, rugged swamp with extruded rubber foliage that needs no maintenance. Fits any space.

Jumbo Swamp Special large size swamp with lots of large chunky weeds and thick grass. Cuts to any size. Will not fray around the edges.

In addition to the above, we have recently started to market 3' x 2' swamp floor tiles. Each tile is made from a tough, rugged, grasslike material and is foam backed for extra hard wearing. There's no waste: simply buy the number of tiles you need to fit the space available. Each tile can be lifted and replaced when necessary.

May we draw your attention to one minor point: the need for correct installation. Incorrectly installed swamps will fray and crack and produce unsightly damp patches along adjoining vegetation.

Yours sincerely,

Clifford Sniggling
Customer Liaison Officer

Dear God,

Thank you for your letter. We do indeed stock geological features suitable for new worlds. You may care to visit our showrooms and inspect the full range of products available.

Of particular interest to your current needs would be our extensive range of monoclinal shifting (lateral erosional activity taking place where a river flows along the strike of a gently dipping rock strata and a less resistant stratum overlies one or more resistances). These are always very popular with amateur creators and no world is complete without one.

I would also like to draw your attention to our superb range of igneous intrusions which are ideal for all climates and are suitable for indoor and outdoor use.

Yours sincerely,

Norman Turgid

Norman Turgid
Sales Officer

"God"

CREATIVE CONSULTANCY PROPERTY SERVICING
Agent for: AMALGAMATED WORLDS Pty.
Registered Office: UNIT 4, LEVEL 2, CENTRAL PLAZA
Telephone: 353 500000 Telex: GOD
Directors: GOD (Managing, Sales, Financial)

Dear Mr. Scrummage,

Re: Creation Of The World

Thank you for your letter. I am sure you will understand me
when I say that I was not a little concerned by its content.
As you will recall, we had made a firm commitment to a
mutually acceptable starting date, so it has come as something
of a shock for me to learn that you now wish that date to
be rearranged.

I am sure you do indeed have 'other things on' and that it
would be 'a bit squiffy' to fit in the required work. But
I must point out that we all have other commitments and the
totally selfish attitude you exhibit is not one I applaud.
Nor, incidentally, do I approve of you referring to me as
'guv'nor'. Keep your familiarities to yourself in future.

I doubt whether any insistence on my behalf that you meet
with your contractual and moral obligations will be met with
a suitable response. I am, anyway, someone who prides himself
on humility and I am therefore reluctant to start throwing
my weight around at this juncture. However, be warned that
I am not at all pleased with this setback and I trust you
will take every step to ensure it does not happen again.
When can we expect you to be ready? I would point out that
this is a matter of the utmost urgency.

Yours insistently,

Veronica Makepiece

pp. God

Dear Mr. Scrummage,

Re: Creation Of The World

Your latest letter has just reached me. Might I suggest
that in future you invest in a postage stamp; from a purely
personal point of view, I always find it achieves a faster
reaction from the postman.

Thank you for letting me know your plans for a new date on
which to start creation. I am sure a week on Tuesday will
be acceptable to us. We had rather hoped that work might
start on Monday and finish on Sunday. We felt that this
would look better in the history books, but as time is short
we are prepared to forego this academic nicety.

Please take this letter as confirmation of the revised date.
I trust we might now look forward to a speedy conclusion of
the work.

Yours sincerely,

Veronica Makepiece

"God"

CREATIVE CONSULTANCY PROPERTY SERVICING
Agent for: AMALGAMATED WORLDS Pty.
Registered Office: UNIT 4, LEVEL 2, CENTRAL PLAZA
Telephone: 353 500000 Telex: GOD
Directors: GOD (Managing, Sales, Financial)

Dear Mr. Scrummage,

Re: Creation of The World

My secretary has just passed to me a letter which she begged
I did not read in front of her. I can see why. The contents
caused me to quite lose control and, had the poor girl been
present, I fear I might indeed have beaten her senseless in
my raging fury.

Yes, you are quite right to suppose I wouldn't be at all
pleased to learn you can't make Tuesday. And yes, I do
consider a long-standing customer's leaking guttering insufficient excuse for your not being able to attend. What is
guttering in comparison with the creation of a world? And
no, I certainly won't accept your abject apologies.

You are, I am sure, fully aware that Amalgamated Worlds are
an extremely large and important company and that the
repercussions resulting from our letting them down are likely
to be enormous. I for my part see no reason why any of the
blame should attach itself to me. You may therefore be
assured that when the proverbial hits the fan - as it inevitably
will - it will be you and not me who faces the wrath of those
concerned.

I trust that in this light of this advice you will now reconsider your decision.

Yours forcefully,

Veronica Makepiece

pp. God

CREATIVE CONSULTANCY PROPERTY SERVICING
Agent for: AMALGAMATED WORLDS Pty.

Registered Office: UNIT 4, LEVEL 2, CENTRAL PLAZA
Telephone: 353 500000 Telex: GOD
Directors: GOD (Managing, Sales, Financial)

Dear Mr. Scrummage,

Re: Creation Of The World

Your latest letter reached me today and I must confess that
I am still far from happy. Thursday may be 'only two days
on' to you, but it represents a considerable delay on the
starting date for which we had originally planned. Moreover,
it now means the work will finish on Wednesday evening -
hardly the most memorable of occasions, and certainly not
one suited to the superb launch party Amalgamated Worlds have
in mind.

However, it is at least (I would now assume) a definite date.
I would far rather work to a schedule which can be relied
upon rather than to some fanciful date you have chosen using
your calendar and a pin. I am therefore forced to accept
your revised schedule. Reluctantly.

I must stress, however, that this new starting date must be
kept at all costs. I will risk considerable scorn in presenting
it to Amalgamated Worlds. You will risk far more if you don't
keep to it.

Yours aggressively,

Veronica Makepiece

ᐟ· God

CREATIVE CONSULTANCY PROPERTY SERVICING
Agent for: AMALGAMATED WORLDS Pty.
Registered Office: UNIT 4, LEVEL 2, CENTRAL PLAZA
Telephone: 353 500000 Telex: GOD
Directors: GOD (Managing, Sales, Financial)

Dear Mr. Scrummage,

Re: Creation Of The World

I have spent the last ten minutes regaining my usual composure
and tidying up a trail of total devastation

After all that was said and written, I find it totally impossible
to conceive how you could have the brass neck to consider asking
for more time. In my last letter I made it perfectly clear that
you were not to delay matters further. Yet here you are unashamedly
announcing that it will now be Sunday before you start work! And
for what reason? You 'have a spot of contract work for a property
company'! I am fully aware, without your smart-alec comments, that
you don't have to pay tax on their work, but I find it impossible
to accept the virtue of this.

Now listen to me. We are fearfully late! We are about to embark upon perhaps
the most memorable project ever! And all you can think about is
some sordid little plan to defraud the taxman!!!

Quite apart from everything else, it will now mean we start work
on Sunday - the one day we had hoped to keep free as a day of
rest. I can only suggest you write back immediately reconsidering
the time schedule, or else start considering yourselves summarily
dismissed.

Yours most aggrievedly,

Veronica Makepiece

PP· God

Dear God,

I am writing with regard to National Insurance on the creation of the world. It is my considered opinion that, although you will be undertaking six days of work (which therefore exceeds the maximum laid down to qualify for assessment as part-time work), you are at the same time also undertaking one week of work (which would therefore fall below the minimum laid down to qualify for full-time work).

I would suggest that in this instance the work be assessed as an open contract which means that employees would be responsible for notifying this office and for paying all National Insurance contributions themselves.

With regard to the one day of rest, I must confess I am unsure whether this should be included as paid holiday, or whether the contract in fact involves only six days of labour, leaving employees contractually free to undertake other work on the seventh day should they so wish. Since you seem keen to impress this as a day of rest I would suggest that perhaps this be written into the contracts of the individuals concerned so that technically there can be no doubt that they are still in your employ on the seventh day and can therefore rightly claim to be resting. That way, even if they do choose to undertake other work on the seventh day, you will still be quite within your rights to claim that on the seventh day they did rest.

I hope that this will clear up the matter to your satisfaction.

Yours sincerely,

Peter Groin

Peter Groin
Information Officer

"god"

CREATIVE CONSULTANCY PROPERTY SERVICING
Agent for: AMALGAMATED WORLDS Pty.
Registered Office: UNIT 4, LEVEL 2, CENTRAL PLAZA
Telephone: 353 500000 Telex: GOD
Directors: GOD (Managing, Sales, Financial)

Dear Mr. Cohen-Cohen,

Re: Creation Of The World

It is with regret that I have to inform you that we still await confirmation of a definite starting date from the builders. I can only apologise for this and trust that you will bear with me for just a trifle longer. I am hoping to receive further information within the next few days and will, of course, be in touch as soon as I have some news.

In the meantime, I thought you might like to see copies of some of the information I have received recently from suppliers regarding fixtures and fittings for the world. I am also enclosing copies of the letters I received from the Office of Patents and the Consolidated National Insurance Office, which I am sure you will find of particular interest.

Perhaps you would care to read through the enclosed and let me have your comments.

Yours sincerely,

Veronica Makepiece

pp. God

OFFICE OF PATENTS*

*Patent applied for

Dear Sir,

Re: Creation Of The World

Thank you for your letter. From the information which you have supplied, I would make the following points:

a) It would not be possible to patent the concept of the world per se. As you know, a large number of planets already exist and the idea of a new planet, or even a new galaxy, could at no time be construed to be sufficiently unique as to afford it patent status.

b) However, it would be possible to patent any specific world in terms of its characteristics. This is a far more limiting patent since it would cover only the sum total of these characteristics, not each individually. For instance, you could not patent a mountain, or even a chain of mountains. You could patent them only as part of the world as a whole.

Basically, I would suggest that when your world is complete you fill out a detailed resume of all aspects concerning size, shape, colour, smell, distinguishing features, distinguishing noises, distinguishing names and any other factors which you feel add intrinsically to the overall concept of the world. It would then be possible to patent these in toto to prevent anyone from copying your ideas.

As I said, this is a far more limiting patent and it would be possible for other creators to subsequently come up with a world very similar to your own without in fact infringing any patents.

I would suggest you bear this in mind and contact me again when your world is complete.

Yours faithfully,

Alison Kalahari

Alison Kalahari
<u>Library</u>

BODYSNATC

Skulls, mandibles, ribs (m. and f.), sternums, verteb

CHIP RESISTANT! HEAT RESIST

Pelvic Girdles
(discontinued line)
Huge reduction. For a new, slimmer
you
(Can be fitted in under 5 minutes!
Needs no washers!)

SPINAL COLUMNS
with new rubberised flanges, vulcanised
sprockets and high-tension
intervertebral discs
(Contains no artificial ingredients)

Skulls
Tough and rugged
Award-winning Design
CLIP-ON

Noses
Choice of shapes
Greek, Roman, Bugner, Manilow
Please state whether stick-on, bolt-on,
screw-on or glue-on fixings required

**Large quantity of warts —
slightly damaged but will repair!**

SELF-ADHESIVE BODY HAIR
Ideal for Italians

HANDS
$2 each or 3 for $5 (fingernails
and tattoos extra)

Gl
lym
so
ar

RIBS
Buy direct from us at well
below shop prices

SOLID CAST IRON

Hernias – Add a touch of elegance to that
body with a strangulated hernia. Many
styles available.

GALL BLADDERS
New special features include:
* stores digestive fluid secreted
  by the liver
* acts as reservoir for bile
Guaranteed against biliary colic
SNAP-ON FITMENT

**All shapes!
All colours!
All conditions!**

ODDMENTS FOR SALE OR RENT
HAMSTRINGS Larynx, muscles,
pelvis, tongue, ear, prostate. Must
sell. Owner going abroad. First to see
will buy.
ABDOMENS Please state preferred
shape. Ideal for women and men.
Also ideal for sheep, cows,
hedgehogs.

Add a
GRO
toe. A
ALI
care
reas
AU
one
AC
te

HERS LTD

lumns, sacrums, scrotums (m. and f.)

! RUST RESISTANT!

TEETH
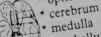

All sizes, all shapes
New and secondhand
new and reconditioned gums
rs: White, yellow, green, red,
natural, tan

Feet
Many unusual features:
Tibion avicullars
Collateral ligaments
Plantar ligaments
Corns
Please state whether left
or right required

BRAINS ☆
Add that touch of luxury with a fully-
fitted brain! Available in four sizes:
small, medium, large, swotty.

Fits all leading makes of head.

Includes ★ olfactory bulb
★ optic nerve
★ cerebrum
★ medulla
★ cerebellum
★ screws and washers

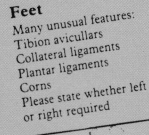

SKIN
Red, white, brown, yellow, black, pink
and ash-grey available

Free estimate

Free fixing and fitting

Free underlay and sebaceous glands

MOUTHS
Don't be confused by
imitations! We
stock the largest range
of mouths.
(Tongues not
included)

A. Uvula.
B. Tonsil.
C. Pillars of the fauces.

ALIMENTARY CANAL

Fits Male and Female
Ideal for all digestive work
Non-regurgitative!
Ulcer-proof!

Complete with pharynx, oesophagus,
stomach, gall bladder, duodenum, small
intestine, colon (ileo-caecal valve extra)

LYMPHATIC SYSTEMS AND SPLEENS
(Large quantity – slightly shop soiled
but otherwise all right)
Ideal for first-time buyer

f realism with an IN-
TOENAIL. Fits any
le.

ARY CANAL Only one
owner from new. No
offer accepted.

CH'S PLEXUS Only
alec owner from new.

S TENDON Needs at-
ould suit jogger.

BLADDER Immaculate condition
throughout. Full maintenance history
available. Genuine reason for sale.

ULCERS Retired businessman has
ulcers for sale. Would suit middle-
aged, overworked, neurotic wreck.

Due to unforeseen objects I have a
large number of **CUTS AND
BRUISES** for sale. Please state quality and quantity when ordering. Ideal
for insurance claims.

Choice
of finishes:
Bone, wood, plastic
cardboard or
chipboard

END OF THE WORLD

Do-it-yourself products and ideas for the home creator

*Macramé Goldfish Bowl Holder Makes any landscape look like a Garden of Eden, and for only *$1.50* (or *$135.75* with the goldfish). Also available: extra-large 'Shark Size': as above, but holds three large sharks comfortably (or five large sharks uncomfortably).

*Knitted Savannah-type Vegetation to make yourself. Comes complete with two knitting needles and 495,000 tons of 4-ply wool. *$2,000* (animals not included)

*Hand-embroidered Great Artesian Basin Rug Measures approximately 2,000 × 1,000 miles. Avoid the expense of real vegetation with this finely woven, hand-embroidered rug (machine-washable). *$994,000*

*Cuddly Felt Urals At last, the space-saving event of the year: cuddly, life-sized Ural Mountains that fold neatly away to form a double bed! Each peak is made from tough, durable, Ordovician-style polyester, with felt slopes and foam rubber filling. *$2,994,179,281* (includes inflatable livestock)

*Wickerwork Igneous Intrusions Just like mother used to make! Tough, attractive, yet surprisingly rugged wickerwork landforms. Everything from volcanic plugs to peneplains available. *From $27 each*

*Delightful Fur-lined River Banks These delightful fur-lined river banks, complete with plastic imitation wildlife, need no maintenance (except for a quick rub over with a damp cloth and an occasional polish with a copy of *Ecology Today*). Simply get them and forget them! Fully flood-proof. *$25 per mile*

*Polystyrene Clouds Quick to assemble, realistic, snap-together clouds made of a tough, durable substance. Hand painted. Hang them from any tall object and they look just like the real thing! *$40* (or *$80* with the special mounting stand)

*Papier-mâché Continents Based on well-loved railway model design, these light and portable giant-sized continents can now be supplied at ridiculous prices ... from as little as *$0.25* each!

END OF THE WORLD NOVELTY GIFT EMPORIUM
Callers always welcome

REG AND WARREN BILBOUS
Vegetation Supplies (Trade Only)

NOW AVAILABLE

Tundra
A very cold, very dull, very icy type of climate. Good for those who like very cold, dull, icy types of climate. Ideal also for those without a deep freeze who want somewhere to keep their food.

Coniferous Forests
Quite cold, quite dull, quite icy ... but with lots of trees. Ideal for tree-fetishists who can't resist the firm young boughs of supple young pine trees as they twist and bend erotically in the wind.

Broad-leaved Forests
Not quite so cold or as icy as above. But still pretty dull. Ideal for deep-water fish who like broad-leaved trees.

Mediterranean Vegetation
Quite nice and pleasant, with lots of vines and sycamores and things like that. Especially ideal for people called Guiseppi and Giovanni ... and things like that.

BEASTIES

Exotic! Unusual! Bizarre! Cheap!

Suppliers of exotic wildlife, exotic wildlife meat pies, exotic wildlife pasties, exotic wildlife cut into bite-sized pieces and placed in a saucepan with onions, milk, water and seasoning (serves 4—6).

The following are available for immediate delivery:

Animals

Hedgehog
Mole
Common shrew
Uncommon shrew
Common weasel
Common badger
Common bodger
Otter
Dead antelope
Skunk
Ferret
Polecat
Nearly-dead goat
Brown hare
Short hare
Body hare
Nasal hare
Very dead rabbit
Flying squirrel
Flying picket
Flying visit (deleted
  due to typing error)
Black rat
Grey rat
Common rat
Dead rat (see also
  Chicken Chow Mein)
Dirty rat
Dormouse
Dorbell
Harvest mouse
Harvest moose

Chocolate moose
Blue whale
Killer whale
Flying whale
Flying whale with
  turbo engines

Birds

Blackbird
Bullfinch
Great bustard
Rotten bustard
Rotten bustard who
  carves you up in
  traffic
Golden eagle
Golden beagle
Golden seagull
Peregrine falcon
Peregrine sparrow
Mallard
Arthur mallard
Goose
Lesser spotted goose
Dead goose
Dead goose with roast
  potatoes
Guillemot
Rook
Jean rook
Ret's have a rook
  (Japanese)
Hedge sparrow
House sparrow

Wheel sparrow
Pigeon
Walter pigeon
Barn owl
Eagle owl
Tern
Terd (deleted due to
  deaf typist)
Deaf typist
Redundant deaf typist
Redundant deaf typist
  seeks work, anything
  considered
Stormy petrel
Last petrel before
  motorway
Pheasant
Unpheasant
Black tern
Sooty tern
Little tern
Good tern
No left tern
My tern
Great tit
Blue tit
Bearded tit
Bearded tit with a
  sexual identity crisis
Robin redtit
Vulture
Stuffed vulture on
  a stick

O'MURPHY'S
The Brain People

Look what we offer you!!!
New and used brains for ALL makes of head

Top quality — Fully tested brains!

Easy fixing — No special skills required!

Intelligence meter — Allows you to monitor the academic rating to which your brain is being subjected. Simply turn the knob to the required setting and the brain will automatically switch off when the level of conversation gets too intelligent!

- -

Please rush me your exciting new brochure! I am particularly interested in:

☐ Brains ☐ Mrs O'T ☐ Radishes ☐ Your company's accounts

Please send me: ☐ 1 ton of literature
                   ☐ 5 tons of literature
                   ☐ small oceangoing liner's worth of literature

Please call ☐ Yes ☐ Yes ☐ Yes

Please send me a free sample ☐ Yes ☐ No (oh, all right then)

Name ....

Age ....

Address ....

Inside leg measurement ....

Look what they say about O'Murphy Brains:

*** They are very clever indeed Mr O'M.

*** It make me think proper Mr O'C.

*** I feel like a new man Mrs O'T.

*** My head hurts Mr O'AP.

*** It does not seem to have improved my radishes in any way Mr O'F.

*** I think it is smashing Mr B'O.

*** Has provided hours of fun and amusement for the children Mr O'TC.

*** Mnjk msjek Msnshef Mnnnn Ms O'Q.

YOUR QUESTIONS ANSWERED

Will it give me a headache? No, only on Sunday mornings.

Can I use Sellotape to stick it in position? Yes, provided you remember which is the sticky side.

Does it come with a guarantee? Yes, but with this brain you won't be able to understand it.

Will it work loose? No, provided you keep perfectly still.

Can I exchange it for a Ford Cortina? Yes, most reputable garages will accept your brain in part-exchange for a Ford Cortina.

Do I need any special tools to fit it? No, only a Black and Decker Powermate.

Preview

$$MCP - Zp^2 \ \sqrt{qv}\ (n-p)o^2\ 1/ZY\ \sqrt{AB^3}$$

$$(pb^2) \quad -\frac{rpm}{201} + 87.215 + \frac{AC}{DC}\left(\frac{r}{z}\right)^2$$

The Mathematical Handbook For All Creators

Edited by:

K.C. CRUMP^2	University of Redbricken
$\sqrt{}$ S.S. STROPPLER	University of Micklewurterbergenstein
J.C.B. BÜLLFELLOW	Löcal Technical College
R.S.V.P. ANTONIONI	University of Humtididdli
P.T.O. $\sqrt{\frac{(ERG)^2}{3}}$	University of Having-A-Good-Time-At-The-Taxpayer's-Expense

Contents
Approx. 9 million figures
      26 million pages
      ISBN 3 + 192 029 7^2
      Published in 27,000 volumes
      Prepublication price approx. 56 million billion dollars
      Comes complete with own 36-ton low-loader for easy carriage

**THE UPSURG-YURIBURG
VERY ACADEMIC PRESS**
(and girly magazine publisher)

This book is essential reading for all those involved in serious research work in the field of creation. Whether as a source of knowledge, or as something nice and heavy to hurl at the cat, this is a book you will find hard to put down (mainly because the cheapo glue we used for the binding is still very tacky).

Each volume has been carefully prepared by a leading team of experts, working under the supervision of yet more experts. And indeed, these experts have to account to a series of super-experts, who meet annually to form committees and panels to look into other areas where experts might be employed. A full list of all those experts participating can be seen on pages 1 to 94,000 in Volume 1.

This lavishly illustrated volume will build up into a splendid collection. Or alternatively into a splendid semi-detached bungalow (each volume comes complete with a trowel and ½ cwt of cement).

Every creator working in the field will be sure to find this an invaluable and essential source of information.

Publication date: As soon as we can get round to it.

POND'S

Pond life for the home creator
Trade enquiries always welcome

Great diving water beetle This beetle has a dome-shaped body, sometimes 1½ inches long, dark green (occasionally almost black) with a stripe of yellow around its edge. It makes a nice crunching sound when you tread on it.

Dragonflies These beautiful insects are harmless and do an immense amount of good by destroying enormous numbers of flies and winged pests. They have gauzy, iridescent wings that softly reflect the beauty of the sunlight as it shimmers gently on them. And they make a particularly satisfying crunching sound when you drive over them in a large steam roller.

Caddisflies Perhaps these remarkable little dears are the most persecuted of all animal life. They are blessed with an elongated, creamy-white body that disintegrates into literally thousands of bits when you drop a 5,000 lb bomb right on top of them.

Water-boatman A small insect seldom more than 1 inch long. Dark brown to black. Lies on the surface of the water, apparently upside-down. Long legs which show a jerky motion. Recognisable by the black triangular plate on the thorax and the total annihilation that takes place when attacked from a range of six inches with a thermonuclear warhead.

Special offers *(discontinued lines)*

GOVERNMENT GIFT BOX
Our selection box includes 12 snails, 3 slugs, 4 toads, 5 vampire bats, 2 stag beetles, 2 leeches and 4 frogs. Comes complete with 5 gallons of stagnant water, fungus, leaf mould, stones for the little creatures to crawl back under, and a soggy rag full of slime.

BAG OF WORMS
Over 5,000 different worms in a shiny black plastic bag! Convert easily into a bag of 10,000 worms (Scissors not included.)

...den's Garden Centre
Wild flowers • Trees
Wild fruits • Grasses • Ferns
Rushes • Fungi

FLOWERS
Marsh grass
Marsh weed
Marsh marigold
Marsh mallow
Deadly nightshade
Deadly lampshade
Pansy
Wild pansy
Absolutely livid pansy
Adder
Puff adder
Puff adder's 'colleague'

MUSHROOMS
Bleeding agaric
Bleeding morel
Morel support
Death cap
Shaggy cap
Andy capp
Bleeding andy capp
Warted agaric
Spotty agaric
Spotty warted agaric
(with a runny nose)

TREES
Horse chestnut
Sweet chestnut
Man-eating chestnut
Lombardy poplar
Ford poplar
Ford poplar 1300E
Giant redwood
Giant redhead
Beech
Palm beech
Yew (Taxus baccata)
Chancellor of Exchequer
(Taxes tabacca)

RUSHES
Common rush
Hard rush
Round fruited rush
Rush anroulette
Rush conway
Toad rush
Bulrush
Mad rush
Last-minute rush

The Royal House of MacLozenge, in conjunction with Massive Rip Offs Ltd., are very, very proud to announce a very, very unique offer: the COUNTRIES OF THE WORLD Limited Edition Set. These are not models or miniatures. They are full-size, fully working countries that you can add to your world. And now, for a very, very limited period, we are able to offer subscribers the chance to purchase a complete, marked, signed set of these countries.

Each country when placed in a prominent position in your world will create a most impressive feature that will cause your guests and friends to exclaim 'Ooh', 'Ah' and 'Cor, I wish those countries were mine'. Not only that, but you can use them in the confidence that they will not scratch, chip, fade or rust.

Imagine the pleasure and pride of owning this truly remarkable collection. A collection that is sure to appreciate in value. Overnight. In fact, most sets appreciate in value in a matter of seconds. Why, even in the short period since you began to read this advertisement, you can bet some lucky blighter has profited by three or four hundred per cent just because he was sensible enough to invest in COUNTRIES OF THE WORLD. In fact, you'd be stupid not to rush out straight away and post off your application form. Ab-

solutely mad.
for your set th
in anguish jus
fer it is.

Each count
craftsman wor
light, with no p
wage. Which is
our ridiculousl
what we were g
was so shockec
told him the pr
heart attack anc

This is the onl
this Special Edit
may be offered
decide to keep
tunities to subscr
ched things. Thu
limited to the tot

All countries ar
shown. The shape
are different to th
honest, they're not
in any way.

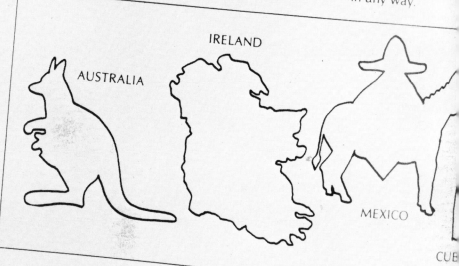

AUSTRALIA

IRELAND

MEXICO

CUB

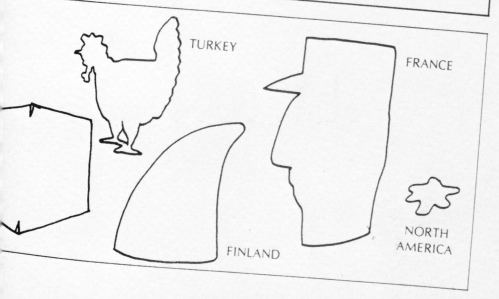

TURKEY

FRANCE

FINLAND

NORTH
AMERICA

AMALGAMATED WORLDS Pty

BIGGEST IN THE UNIVERSE

AMALGAMATED WORLDS PTY
AMALGAMATED WORLDS CORPORATION HOUSE
AMALGAMATED WORLDS CORPORATION PLAZA
AMALGAMATED WORLDS CORPORATION AVENUE
AMALGAMATED WORLDS CORPORATION VILLE

TELEPHONE: 964359214 to 954359792 (inclusive)
TELEX: AMALWORLDS

Dear God,

Re: Creation of World

Many thanks for sending me all the information about supplies
for the world. You certainly seem to have been busy, but I
notice that you've been keeping rather quiet about next
Sunday's starting date.

Perhaps you could drop me a quick line just to confirm that
all is proceeding as planned.

With very best wishes,

T.G. Cohen-Cohen

T.G. Cohen-Cohen
Project Development Officer

"god"

CREATIVE CONSULTANCY PROPERTY SERVICING
Agent for: AMALGAMATED WORLDS Pty.
Registered Office: UNIT 4, LEVEL 2, CENTRAL PLAZA
Telephone: 353 500000 Telex: GOD
Directors: GOD (Managing, Sales, Financial)

Dear Mr. Scrummage,

Re: Creation of The World

May I point out that I am _still_ awaiting confirmation that
you are ready to start work next Sunday. It may have
escaped your notice that today is Wednesday. And it may
therefore also have escaped your notice that we are now only
a matter of days from the start of the creation.

It is essential you confirm this date immediately. Amalgamated
Worlds are naturally concerned that the work will begin on
Sunday, and I am equally anxious to assure them that this is
so.

Yours concernedly,

Veronica Makepiece

PP. God

CROOKED & BENT
Solicitors, Commissioners for Oaths, Licensed Betting Shop

Dear Mr. Slagworthy,

Re: Creation Of The World

We act as solicitors for Mr. God, who has asked that we contact you with regard to the above-named project for which I believe your firm has been contracted as builders.

Mr. God is considerably alarmed at the breach of a contract - a contract to which, I may add, you were a signatory - and which gives reference to all conditions relating to the hereinsobeforementioned subject. And, indeed, it would appear from all discussions which have taken place that you are in flagrant breach of this contract and that legally you are in an invidious position.

Mr. God fears that a legal settlement of the issue may be the only solution now available to him, and he has suggested we write to you to point this out and to urge that you reconsider your position in the matter.

As solicitors it is not our normal practice to offer free legal advice to our clients' adversaries. However, in this instance we make exception to this, if only to impress upon you the utter hopelessness of the position you are now in. We would suggest that without delay you re-examine all aspects of this issue and consider whether you cannot offer a suitable response.

In particular, we would draw your attention to:

1. Your reference to possible fraudulent practice in the offer of low prices in return for cash settlements for work done.
2. The unnatural practices and behaviour called for in your specifications and worksheets that would appear to contravene health and safety requirements.
3. Your continued failure to commence work, and your flagrant breach of agreements made as to the timing of such work.

May I therefore expect your immediate reply.

Your legally, P.P. Scribbling

P.P. Scribbling (Partner)

& UNIVERSAL CONSTRUCTION CO.
General Builders & Contractors

3rd Arch Along
Limepit Viaduct
Telephone 18194804612 (one line)
Telex CONU

MEMBER OF THE FEDERATION OF SMALL BUILDERS
AND BUILDING CONTRACTORS

God,

Re: Creation of The World

I very much regret to inform you that my colleague, Mr Scrummage, no longer with us, since an unfortunate misunderstanding with the ...xman has necessitated his leaving our employ rather hurriedly. I must ...ress that in no way was our good firm implied, and that the incident ... fact involved some 'extra' work Mr Scrummage had undertaken in his own ...ime and which he seemingly forgot to report to the local tax inspector. ...egrettably, these matters do have an unhappy habit of blowing up out of all proportion and it was felt that Mr Scrummage might benefit from a long holiday abroad, if you take my meaning.

As a result of Mr Scrummage's hasty departure I am assuming responsibility for all work undertaken by him which has as yet not reached completion. I regret I was not acquainted with your particular case until now, and was therefore somewhat concerned on opening your file to see that a certain amount of friction appears to have been caused during Mr Scrummage's time with the company. It is my earnest wish to remove these unfortunate tensions and to ensure all business is conducted in a pleasant and cordial manner from now on. I will therefore be at pains to ensure you receive the fullest possible service.

However, just for the moment I must beg you to bear with me. Clearly, with Mr Scrummage no longer with us, we are finding it difficult to keep up with our many commitments and I must therefore warn you that the Sunday date does seem highly unlikely. I would envisage that in two or three weeks we will have a much clearer idea as to where we stand and I will contact you again then to report further.

I trust this will meet with your approval.

Yours soothingly,

X

Ted Slagworthy
Cosmic & Universal Construction Co

COSMIC & UNIVERSAL CONSTRUCTION CO.
General Builders & Contractors

3rd Arch Along
Limepit Viaduct
Telephone 18194804612 (one line)
Telex CONU

MEMBER OF THE FEDERATION OF SMALL BUILDERS
AND BUILDING CONTRACTORS

Dear God,

Re: Creation of The World

I have just received the letter from your solicitor, and confess
I was somewhat upset by its tone. I did assure you we are making every
effort to attend to your work, and I had hoped you would not feel it
necessary to employ a solicitor to this end.

I am now in the process of working through our order book and
would anticipate starting work on your world four weeks from today.
Perhaps you would let me know if that would be convenient for you.

Yours huffily,

Gwyn MacTaggart (Secretary)

pp Ted Slagworthy
Cosmic & Universal Construction Co

"god"
CREATIVE CONSULTANCY PROPERTY SERVICING
Agent for: AMALGAMATED WORLDS Pty.
Registered Office: UNIT 4, LEVEL 2, CENTRAL PLAZA
Telephone: 353 500000 Telex: GOD
Directors: GOD (Managing, Sales, Financial)

Dear Mr. Slagworthy,

Re: Creation of The World

I'm afraid four weeks is totally out of the question. This
work should have been started and finished weeks ago. I
am already in the embarrassing position of having to approach
our customer, Amalgamated Worlds, to let them know that the
work has yet to be started. To compound this by telling them they
may still have to wait a month to see anything for their money
is totally unthinkable.

You'd better rethink your position and give me a ring right
this minute.

Yours crossly,

Veronica Makepiece

pp. God

CROOKED & BENT

Solicitors, Commissioners for Oaths, Licensed Betting Shop

Dear Mr. Slagworthy,

Re: Creation of the World

Once again Mr. God has asked that I write to you about the breach of the contract to which you were a signatory. He has asked me to point out that, if you are not prepared to reconsider your position in the matter, he will have no option but to instruct us to serve notice that we intend to sue.

I trust you will therefore assume from this letter that Mr. God is no longer prepared to tolerate delay and is now taking legal advice with regard to court proceedings. I would be grateful if on receipt of this letter you would contact my office to discuss your considered position. Failure to do so will be assumed to imply your continued intransigence and notice will therefore be served upon you.

Yours accusingly,

P.P. Scribbling

P.P. Scribbling (Partner)

Telephone Message

TIME RECEIVED 3.30pm.   DATE

FROM COS. + UNIV. CONST. CO.

MR. SLAGWORTHY PHONED WHILE YOU WERE OUT. APOLOGISED BUT NO CHANCE OF ALTERING THE DATE. ASKED HIM IF THERE WAS ANY OTHER NEWS BUT PHONE WENT DEAD BEFORE HE COULD REPLY. ASSUME HE RAN OUT OF COINS.

RECEIVED BY V.

COSMIC & UNIVERSAL CONSTRUCTION CO.
General Builders & Contractors

3rd Arch Along
Limepit Viaduct
Telephone 18194804612 (one line)
Telex CONU

MEMBER OF THE FEDERATION OF SMALL BUILDERS
AND BUILDING CONTRACTORS

Dear God,

I was disappointed to receive yet another letter from your solicitor regarding the starting date for the creation of the world. As you will realise, the building trade is of necessity somewhat flexible, and to be held to strict dates and schedules is irksome and impractical and does no one any good.

Please be patient. Quite apart from the fact that we are now under-staffed, we have got a big job on at the moment which I promised to complete last year. After that a couple of loft conversions. Then a damp course. Then you.

I will write again just as soon as possible. Meanwhile, don't rush off and start telling any more tales to your solicitor.

Yours sincerely,

Gwen MacTaggart (Secretary)

123498 CONU G

112 GOD G

ATTN: TED SLAGWORTHY

AM AFRAID LATEST LETTER TOTALLY UNACCEPTABLE. IT IS QUITE
ESSENTIAL THAT THE WORLD BE STARTED WITHIN THE WEEK. I
CANNOT KEEP AMALGAMATED WORLDS WAITING ANY LONGER AND FEAR
MY STANDING WITH THEM WILL BE SEVERELY ERODED UNLESS I CAN
OFFER THEM IMMEDIATE SATISFACTION.
TELEX SOONEST.

GOD

Telephone Message

TIME RECEIVED 2.30pm   DATE _____

FROM Cos. + Univ. Const. Co.

MR. SLAGWORTHY (COSMIC + UNIVERSAL)
PHONED WHILE YOU WERE OUT AT THE
OSTEOPATH. HAS RECEIVED YOUR TELEX.
WILL START TWO WEEKS ON
WEDNESDAY.

RECEIVED BY Veronica

123498 CONU G

112 GOD G

ATTN: TED SLAGWORTHY

TWO WEEKS ON WEDNESDAY NOT ACCEPTABLE. EARLIER DATE OR

WILL SEEK ALTERNATIVE BUILDER. REPLY REQUIRED IMMEDIATEST.

GOD

Telephone Message

TIME RECEIVED 3.30pm DATE _____

FROM COS. + UNIV. CONST. CO.

MR. SLAGWORTHY PHONED WHILE
YOU WERE OUT AT THE CHEMIST'S
GETTING OSTEOPATH'S PRESCRIPTION
RECEIVED LATEST TELEX. SUGGEST
WEEK-ON-TUESDAY INSTEAD.

RECEIVED BY Veronica

Telephone Message

TIME RECEIVED 3.35pm.

FROM OSTEOPATH DATE _____

OSTEOPATH PHONED !
MOST IMPORTANT - HE GAVE YOU THE
WRONG PRESCRIPTION! ON NO ACCOUNT
USE LINAMENT! EFFECTS UNKNOWN.!
MEANT FOR CATTLE ! PLEASE CALL FOR
NEW PRESCRIPTION.

RECEIVED BY Veronica

...NU G

112 GOD G

ATTN: TED SLAGWORTHY

WEEK-ON-MONDAY LATEST POSSIBLE DATE THAT CAN BE ACCEPTED.
AGREE OR DEAL OFF.

GOD

Telephone Message

TIME RECEIVED 4.30pm. DATE _____

FROM COS. + UNIV. CONST. CO.

MR. SLAGWORTHY PHONED WHILE YOU
WERE IN TOILET TRYING TO TAKE
SWELLING DOWN WITH CREAM.
RELUCTANT, BUT ACCEPT DATE !
WILL START MONDAY WEEK.

RECEIVED BY Veronica

Veronica

Would you please place the attached advertisement in a prominent position in the ~~relevant~~ relevant trade journals and ring the estate agent with a view to locating more sizeable office accommodation than this place. Have just popped out to the sweet shop

G

Dear Sir or Madam,

   I am 36, highly intelligent, suave, incredibly attractive, smartly dressed and extremely modest. I would like to be considered for your

Dear Sir or Madam,

I am a 16-year-old schoolgirl and would like to be considered for the position of Person Friday for your

Dear Sir,

Creation of the World

   I am an 83-year-old schoolgirl and I would be like to be considered for the position of Person Friday for the above

Dear Sirs,

Re: Your Advertisement

I was an 83-year-old schoolgirl until I discovered genetic engineering. Now I am an 83-year-old wombat called Terry and

r Sir,

Re: Creation Of The World (Person Friday)

   I wonder if you would be prepared to consider me for the above position. I have been interested in Creation for a number of years, and have myself done a considerable amount of research into animal and plant anatomy.

   I have my own chain saw and mallet together with a twelve bore

Dear Sir,

PERSON FRIDAY VACANCY

I wonder if you would be willing to consider me for your position for Person Friday. I am tall, blonde, good looking, and have this incredible sexy body that just turns men on. And my name is Michael.

Willmotts Vegetation

ORDER

Your order of three (3) weeds is dispatched herewith. All weeds should be planted immediately and not left in the old sock supplied herewith. To propagate these weeds, please read the instructions carefully.

Terms C.O.D.   160.00 Universal $

INTERNATIONAL SUPPLY COMPANY LTD

...e of this great
...r attention th...

Dear God,

Please find enclosed our largest Dodo. We do apologise for the unfortunate spelling mistake in our previous order and trust that you will return the offending sexual aid to us in the enclosed black plastic bin-liner.

Please remit within 30 days. $841.00
                                    84.00
                                  $925.00

OSCAR'S ANIMALS WILD ANIMALS

We supply herewith a selection from our range of Bengali Tigers. As you will no doubt appreciate, Bengali Tigers are not particularly easy things to pack and I'm afraid that in this case we had considerable trouble getting the wretched things to stay still long enough for us to tie the wrapping paper down. Might I suggest that in light of this you perhaps keep a revolver handy when unpacking.

Universal $

(Terms strictly 7 day)
TIGERS (three)   100.00
VET   58.00
VAT   6.00

        TOTAL   164.00

THINGS ON EARTH

INVOICE

Please find herewith your order for 1 (one) skunk (medium/small). We suggest you don't open the airtight bag downwind, and as an added precaution you might like to consider employing someone with a heavy cold to do the job for you. Should you wish to return the skunk to us for any reason, would you please use a sealed plastic bag and mark the package 'SKUNK', otherwise it will upset the girls in our packaging department.

Terms (one month)   Skunk $25.00
                    Airtight box   1.00
                    Second airtight   1.00
                    box   0.50
                    Airtight bag   3.00
                    VAT

                                    $30.50

                    TOTAL

Veronica.

Another enormous bundle of mail (attached) came in today. I have tried hard to sift through most of it. Just throw the rest in a filing cabinet and we'll sort it out at some future date.

In addition, I've filled in the insurance declaration the revised ms-contract, the tax exemption certificates, the employee ~~as~~ credit transfer forms and the daily dockets. I have also filled in an even larger batch of material which I know nothing about but which I thought it best to complete. Everything else I have simply signed and left for you to fill in the details. It's all getting ~~too~~ much for me.

Perhaps things will calm down a bit after building work actually begins next Monday.

Please photocopy the attached letter from Mr Cohen-Cohen at Amalgamated Worlds and forward it to my psychiatrist for analysis (he does a postal service). I suspect Mr C-C. may be suffering some sort of breakdown as a result of the pressure recently. I suspect he's not going to be the only one if things carry on like this.

Have just popped out to the chemist to get something for the weekend.

In haste,

G

AMALGAMATED WORLDS Pty
BIGGEST IN THE UNIVERSE

AMALGAMATED WORLDS PTY
AMALGAMATED WORLDS CORPORATION HOUSE
AMALGAMATED WORLDS CORPORATION PLAZA
AMALGAMATED WORLDS CORPORATION AVENUE
AMALGAMATED WORLDS CORPORATION VILLE

TELEPHONE: 964359214 to 954359792 (inclusive)
TELEX: AMALWORLDS

Dear God,

Recreation of The World

I'm afraid This letter has been particularly

It seems rather The more thing becoming too much afraid to admit. These delays are not good & causing me anguish but maybe it's something I ate or drank too much. Hate to Think how much. Must be gallons.

But to the point of this which was that the migraines as well are getting to me. Doctor keeps giving me pills to take with water – but no water in desk drawer – take with whisky instead – plenty of whisky in drawer.

what was I saying. Oh yes. The world's fine. How do I know? I don't, but think I used to. Once. Can't wait to see the world now That it's finished.

Yours ramblingly,

who am I?

Directors
R.V. Goldstein, B.M. Cohen, B.M.V. Schmidstein,
D.F.C. Rubenstein, R.F. Goldschmidt, T.G. Cohen-Cohen
A.N.O.T.P.K.L. Freiburger, B.K. Jacobstein, H.L. Samuels

"GOD"

CREATIVE CONSULTANCY PROPERTY SERVICING
Agent for: AMALGAMATED WORLDS Pty.
Registered Office: UNIT 4, LEVEL 2, CENTRAL PLAZA
Telephone: 353 500000 Telex: GOD
Directors: GOD (Managing, Sales, Financial)

Dear Mr. Cohen-Cohen,

Re: Creation Of The World

Thank you for all your recent letters. I must say I do agree with what you said about the chickens. I certainly wouldn't doubt their strength and would imagine they could well rip a man apart limb from limb.

That aside, I thought I should also write to inform you that we are at long last ready. It is Friday evening and my desk is cleared ready for the big day next week. I must say it was touch and go whether we would get through all the paper-work on time but I am now confident that, with all that behind us, we can look forward to an easier ride. I have myself arranged to take a short weekend break away before work begins on Monday. There is little else to finish here and I feel I have earned the rest. I shall, however, be back in the office on Monday morning should you wish to contact me. I trust this will be in order.

Returning to the other matter you raised in your most recent letter, I would suggest that the easiest way to rid yourself of the bogeyman, should he indeed be after you, is plenty of rest and a little less alcohol. I do indeed agree that three bottles of malt whisky a day will encourage the bogey to come after you.

God,

I have spoken with the travel agent who confirms all details as follows:

2 nights B.+B. at Shadey Glenn Guest House single room (H.+C.)

Proprietors Mr. & Mrs. Eric Flange.

By overnight bus (leaves bus station 5.30 pm)

Veronica

123498 CONU G
112 GOD G

ATTN: TED SLAGWORTHY

MONDAY 9.27 A.M.

TOOK OPPORTUNITY TO VISIT SITE TODAY (MONDAY) TO WISH YOU
WELL ON PROJECT. ASTONISHED TO FIND NO ONE THERE!
PLEASE REMEMBER WE HAVE ONLY SIX = REPEAT SIX = DAYS IN
WHICH TO COMPLETE WORK. IMPERATIVE YOU DO NOT DELAY.
PLEASE TELEX YOUR SOONEST REPLY

GOD

112
1234

123498 CONU G
112 GOD G

ATTN: TED SLAGWORTHY

MONDAY
1.15 P.M.

STILL NO REPLY TO PREVIOUS TELEX! REPEAT IT IS VITAL WE
DO NOT DELAY. PLEASE TELEX TO CONFIRM YOU ARE ABLE TO
COMPLETE ON TIME.

GOD

112 GOD G
123498 CONU G

123498 CONU G
112 GOD G

ATTN: ANYBODY

MONDAY
3.30 P.M.

AM EXTREMELY WORRIED REGARDING PROGRESS OF
OUR PROJECT. ESSENTIAL WE MEET DATE OR THE
CONTRACT INVALID. IN CASE YOU DON'T UNDER-
STAND, THIS MEANS NO = REPEAT = NO MONEY.

PLEASE TELEX RIGHT NOW.

MOST URGENT.

GOD

112 GOD G
123498 CONU G

123498 CONU G
112 GOD G

ATTN: TED SLAGWORTHY

MONDAY
4.45 P.M.

MY SECRETARY HAS TELEPHONED FROM SITE AND CONFIRMS
NO WORK BEGUN. MOST SERIOUS. WOULD CONFIRM THAT
TODAY YOU WERE TO DIVIDE LIGHT FROM DARKNESS. LIGHT
TO BE CALLED DAY AND DARKNESS TO BE CALLED NIGHT.

WOULD REMIND YOU THAT YOU ARE UNDER LEGAL OBLIGATION
TO COMPLY WITH TERMS OF CONTRACT.
MUST ASSUME YOU NOW INTEND TO COMPLETE ALL WORK IN
FIVE DAYS. IS THIS CORRECT? IF SO PLEASE CONFIRM
THIS CAN STILL BE DONE. WE REMAIN DOUBTFUL. YOUR
TELEX REPLY TO BE ON MY DESK TOMORROW MORNING WITHOUT
FAIL.

GOD

112 GOD G
123498 CONU G

ATTN: TED SLAGWORTHY

TUESDAY

10.00 A.M.

AM FRANKLY APPALLED TO FIND NO WORK STILL BEGUN ON MY
CREATION AND NO REPLY TO YESTERDAY'S TELEXES AWAITING.
VISITED SITE THIS MORNING (TUESDAY) FULLY EXPECTING
TO FIND WORK IN PROGRESS. ASTOUNDED TO DISCOVER NO
SIGN OF ACTIVITY.

TELEPHONE OR TELEX NOW OR CONSIDER PROJECT IN JEOPARDY.

GOD

TUESDAY
11.45 A.M.

AM STILL AWAITING YOUR REPLY. THIS REALLY IS BEYOND
THE PALE.

WOULD POINT OUT THAT TODAY YOU ARE DUE TO DIVIDE
WATERS THAT ARE UNDER FIRMAMENT, IN ADDITION TO
DIVISION OF LIGHT FROM DARKNESS WHICH YOU NEGLECTED
YESTERDAY.

WOULD DRAW YOUR ATTENTION TO PENALTY CLAUSE IN
CONTRACT.

GOD

112 GOD G
123498 CONU G

God

Ted Slagworthy phoned
while you were out at lunch.
Very apologetic — said not to get
in a flap — would finish work w
sweat by Friday evening at lates
Sorry for delay — has had to fin
off one or two outstanding jobs...
(then the pips went)

Veronica

ATTN: TED SLAGWORTHY

TUESDAY
2.30 P.M.

HAVE BEEN HANDED YOUR PHONE MESSAGE WHICH CAME THROUGH
WHILE I WAS AT LUNCH. TRIED TO PHONE BACK BUT EACH
TIME GOT THE ENGAGED TONE. ASSUME YOU HAVE TAKEN IT
OFF HOOK.
FRANKLY NOT CONVINCED YOU WILL GET WORK DONE ON TIME.
AND AM AS STONED = SORRY, ASTOUNDED = THAT YOU SHOULD
TAKE ON OTHER WORK AT SUCH AN IMPORTANT TIME.
HAVE ACCORDINGLY INSTRUCTED MY BANKERS TO STOP ALL
FURTHER PAYMENTS TO YOUR ACCOUNT UNTIL SATISFACTORY
PROGRESS IS ESTABLISHED.
CONTACT ME AGAIN IMMEDIATELY OR CONSIDER YOURSELF IN
BREACH OF CONTRACT.

GOD

G.

Mr. Slagworthy of Cos + Univ. Const. Co.
phoned (again).
Seemed rather cross - muttered something
awfully rude - asked him to repeat it
but wouldn't.
Seemed very upset about "the readies"
(money?)
Said they would start work late this
afternoon and would have job finished
as promised.
Said something about keeping a "Bee
in your Bonnet" (?)
Asked if he'd like to speak to you
personally — rang off.
Veronica

ATTN: TED SLAGWORTHY

TUESDAY
3.45 P.M.

HAVE RECEIVED YOUR LATEST TELEPHONE MESSAGE. EXPECTED
TO SPEAK PERSONALLY BUT MY SECRETARY SAYS YOU SEEMED
BUSY AND DID NOT HAVE TIME TO WAIT.
DOUBT THIS VERY MUCH AND ASSUME IT WAS MERELY RELUCTANCE
TO FACE UP TO YOUR RESPONSIBILITIES. I NOTE THAT YOU
NOW INTEND TO START WORK LATE THIS AFTERNOON AND CONTINUE
SOLIDLY FOR REST OF WEEK.
AFRAID I DO NOT SHARE YOUR OPTIMISM AND WILL CONTINUE
TO SUSPEND PAYMENTS UNTIL AM ASSURED YOU CAN STILL
COMPLETE ALL WORK IN WHAT IS NOW FOUR AND A QUARTER DAYS.

EXPECTING TO HEAR FROM YOU SHORTLY.

OD

ATTN: GOD

TUESDAY
4.30 P.M.

HAVE STARTED WORK. DIVIDED LIGHT FROM DARKNESS AND
DIVIDED WATERS UNDER FIRMAMENT. HAVE ALSO GATHERED
TOGETHER THE WATERS UNDER THE HEAVEN UNTO ONE PLACE
AND MADE A START ON BRINGING FORTH GRASS, THE HERB
YIELDING SEED AND THE FRUIT TREE YIELDING FRUIT
AFTER HIS KIND.

TRUST THIS NOW ALLOWS YOU TO INSTRUCT YOUR BANKERS
TO REINSTATE PAYMENTS.

REGARDS

TED SLAGWORTHY
COSMIC & UNIVERSAL CONSTRUCTION CO

TUESDAY
4.45 P.M.

HAVE RECEIVED YOUR TELEX WHICH QUITE FRANKLY
STAGGERS ME. YOUR CLAIM TO HAVE COMPLETED
VIRTUALLY THE FIRST THREE DAYS' CREATION IN
LITTLE UNDER AN HOUR IS ONE I CANNOT ENTERTAIN.
AT THAT RATE YOU WOULD BE ABLE TO COMPLETE THE
WHOLE WORLD IN JUST TWO HOURS.

WILL VISIT SITE THIS EVENING (TUESDAY) TO
INSPECT FOR MYSELF. UNTIL THEN WILL CONTINUE
TO WITHHOLD PAYMENTS.

GOD

123498 CONU G
112 GOD G

ATTN: T. SLAGWORTHY

WEDNESDAY
9.45 A.M.

TOOK THE LIBERTY OF VISITING SITE LAST NIGHT
(TUESDAY) TO CHECK ON YOUR CLAIMS AND IT WAS AS I
HAD SUSPECTED. VIRTUALLY NONE OF THE WORK YOU
CLAIMED FOR HAS BEEN DONE. I FOUND ONLY A LITTLE
PATCH OF LIGHT THAT YOU APPEARED TO HAVE DIVIDED
FROM THE DARKNESS AND A FEW HERBS.
OF COURSE, AS THERE WAS NO LIGHT IT WAS DIFFICULT
TO INSPECT MUCH ELSE BUT I CERTAINLY COULDN'T SEE
ANY DIVIDED WATERS, NOR WERE WATERS GATHERED
TOGETHER.
MY SECRETARY HAS BEEN DISPATCHED TO REPORT. WILL
CONTACT FURTHER WHEN HER FINDINGS ARE KNOWN.

GOD

112 GOD G
123498 CONU G

Progress   Wednesday

1. ~~All~~ very little Lightness
2. Waters not gathered.
3. Only three herbs spotted.
4. Gardener installing herbs (a ~~sex~~ maniac)
5. Smell of gas.
6. Damp patches on firmament.
7. Electricity not working.
8. Litter everywhere
9. Portaloo on site not working
10. No grass.
11. No trees
12. No creatures tha creepeth!
13. Mountains wrong size!!

123498 CONU G
112 GOD G

WEDNESDAY
12.15 P.M.

HAVE NOW SPOKEN TO MY SECRETARY WHO VISITED SITE
AND APPEARS TO BE IN MUCH DISTRESS. NOT ONLY DID SHE
HAVE TO WADE ABOUT KNEE-DEEP IN WATER IN SEMI-
DARKNESS BUT THE PERSON YOU EMPLOYED TO BRING FORTH
GRASS AND HERB YIELDING SEED AFTER HIS KIND VERY
NEARLY MOLESTED HER AND SHE HAD TO LEAVE HURRIEDLY.

FROM WHAT LITTLE OF THE POOR GIRL'S ACCOUNT I COULD
FOLLOW BETWEEN HER SOBS IT SEEMS YOUR CLAIMS WERE
AS FANCIFUL AS I HAD FEARED.

AM THEREFORE CONTINUING TO WITHHOLD ALL PAYMENTS
AND HAVE ALSO TAKEN LEGAL ADVICE.

        GOD

            112 GOD G
            123498 CONU G

123498 CONU G
112 GOD G

ATTN: TED SLAGWORTHY

WEDNESDAY
3.35 P.M

MY SECRETARY HAVING GONE OFF EARLY TO RECOVER I
HAVE BEEN COMPELLED TO LOOK AFTER OFFICE. YOU
CAN IMAGINE MY SHOCK WHEN I INADVERTENTLY SWITCHED
ON THE TELEPHONE ANSWERING MACHINE AND HEARD YOUR
VOICE. RARELY HAVE I HEARD SUCH LANGUAGE. I
WOULD MOST CERTAINLY HAND OVER CONTENTS TO POLICE
FOR INVESTIGATION WERE I LESS CHARITABLE. THINK
YOURSELF LUCKY I AM.

MAY I PERHAPS PUT YOU RIGHT ON A FEW FACTS THAT YOUR
STREAM OF ABUSE SEEMED TO NEGLECT.
FIRSTLY, YOU CONTRACTED TO SUPPLY ME WITH A WORLD OF
SPECIFIED DESIGN WITHIN SIX DAYS. SECONDLY, YOU
AGREED TO FOLLOW A MUTUALLY CONVENIENT PROGRESS
CHART AND TO NOTIFY THIS OFFICE IF FOR ANY REASON
YOU WERE UNABLE TO MEET SPECIFIED DATES. YOU HAVE
CLEARLY FAILED ON BOTH POINTS. AND NO AMOUNT OF
SLANDEROUS ILL-MOUTHED BAR-ROOM FILTH WILL PUT
MATTERS STRAIGHT.

I AWAIT YOUR IMMEDIATE APOLOGY.

        GOD

            112 GOD G
            123498 CONU G

112 GOD G
123498 CONU G

ATTN: GOD

THURSDAY
9.30 A.M.

SORRY ABOUT OUTBURST YESTERDAY. WAS QUITE WRONG OF
ME, AND IT WON'T HAPPEN AGAIN.

AM UNDER ENORMOUS PRESSURE OF LATE, AND NOT JUST FROM
CREATION OF YOUR WORLD. WOULD ORDINARILY HAVE HAD YOUR
WORLD STITCHED UP BY NOW, BUT SEEMS TO HAVE COME AT A
DIFFICULT TIME. IN ADDITION, AND I KNOW THIS ISN'T
REALLY ANY OF YOUR BUSINESS, MY WIFE HAS RECENTLY LEFT
ME FOR ANOTHER MAN, AND I HAVE BEEN FORCED TO LOOK AFTER
MY FOUR SMALL CHILDREN, ALL OF WHOM ARE UNDER FIVE AND
REQUIRE CONSTANT ATTENTION. ESPECIALLY THE SMALLEST WHO
IS JUST RECOVERING FROM A NEAR-FATAL ACCIDENT.

BUT.YOU DON'T WANT TO HEAR OF MY PROBLEMS. WHY SHOULD
YOU CARE,JUST BECAUSE MY WIFE HAS THROWN A LIFETIME'S
DEVOTED LOVE BACK IN MY FACE AND LEFT ME A BROKEN MAN.

SORRY. I WAS GETTING CARRIED AWAY.

REST ASSURED WE'RE DOING OUR BEST UNDER DIFFICULT
CIRCUMSTANCES TO COMPLETE WORK ON TIME.

REGARDS

TED SLAGWORTHY

123498 CONU G
112 GOD G

"god"

CREATIVE CONSULTANCY PROPERTY SERVICING
Agent for: AMALGAMATED WORLDS Pty.

Registered Office: UNIT 4, LEVEL 2, CENTRAL PLAZA
Telephone: 353 500000 Telex: GOD
Directors: GOD (Managing, Sales, Financial)

Dear Mr. Slagworthy,

Re: Creation of The World

Thank you for your long and touching telex. While
offering you any amount of compassion and sympathy,
I'm afraid no amount of heart-rending misfortune can
prevent me from commenting upon the abysmal scene
which I encountered this morning (Thursday).

I visited the site then on my way to the office, and
was optimistically entertaining the fanciful notion
that I might see someone working. I was <u>not</u> expecting to see everyone and everything floating in 10 feet
of deep thick slime. Some other pertinent points
which I noted were :

      1. Land in the wrong place
      2. No hills
      3. Only one fish
      4. Gross irregularities in
         employees' pension and
         insurance contributions.

In addition, the mountains (both of them) had been installed
upside-down; all three rivers ran uphill; and what remained
of the insects appeared to have been assembled with nuts
and bolts.

As you are well aware, this appalling debacle is not at
all what was requested. I insist that you pull yourself
together and knuckle down to some hard graft. I am sending my secretary over to the site this morning for another
progress report.

Yours,

Veronica Makepiece

pp. God

P.S. Re the agreed schedule (section 7 (B)/1 paragraph 8 line
31. For 'Russian Urinals to be 2,000 miles long', substitute
'Russian Urals to be 2,000 miles long'.

P.P.S. I suggest you ring 'Contact-o-Pair' for an au pair if all
this guff about your four small children is true.

112 GOD G

ATTN: GOD

THURSDAY

12.30 P.M.

ARRIVED AT SITE AT 11.15 TO FIND WORKMEN HAVING A CUP OF
TEA. SAID THEY HAD JUST THAT MINUTE STOPPED WORK.
COULD SEE NO SIGN OF ACTIVITY. ASKED VARIOUS SEARCHING
QUESTIONS, BUT THEY PRETENDED TO BE FOREIGN AND SAID
'QUE?' A LOT .

EVERYONE HAS GONE TO LUNCH NOW. WILL REPORT AGAIN
THIS AFTERNOON .

VERON

112 GOD G

ATTN: GOD

THURSDAY
3.35 P.M.

RETURNED TO SITE AT 2.30 TO FIND NO ONE HAD RETURNED
FROM LUNCH. RETURNED AT 3.00. STRONG SMELL OF BEER
ABOUT, AND THE WORKMEN WERE HAVING ANOTHER CUP OF TEA.
SAID 'HOW CURIOUS YOU ALWAYS SEEM TO COME JUST
AFTER WE'VE DONE A PARTICULARLY STRENUOUS BIT OF
WORK'. ASKED THEM MORE SEARCHING QUESTIONS BUT
THEY JUST PACKED UP AND WENT HOME.

VERONICA

112 GOD G

123498 CONU G
112 GOD G

ATTN: TED SLAGWORTHY

THURSDAY
3.50 P.M.

APPALLING REPORTS ABOUT THE SITE FROM MY SECRETARY.
DEMAND YOU TAKE THE SITUATION IN HAND WITHOUT FAIL
OR ALL HELL WILL BE LET LOOSE.

GOD

---

112 GOD G
123498 CONU G

ATTN: GOD

THURSDAY
4.20 P.M.

SORRY TO HEAR YOU'RE NOT HAPPY. SUGGEST YOU DON'T WORRY.
SUGGEST YOU KEEP AL HELL CHAINED UP. SUGGEST YOU
INSTRUCT YOUR BANKERS TO REINSTATE PAYMENTS. SUGGEST
YOU TAKE A NICE LONG HOLIDAY AS IT'S OBVIOUSLY ALL
GETTING TOO MUCH FOR YOU.

KIND REGARDS.

TED

123498 CONU G
112 GOD G

ATTN: T.G. COHEN-COHEN

FRIDAY
9.15 A.M.

WORLD COMING ON PRETTY WELL. SLIGHT DELAY OVER ONE OR
TWO ITEMS BUT OTHERWISE NO PROBLEMS. JUST WHAT WE ALL
HAD IN MIND. EVERYTHING LOOKING REALLY GOOD AND THINK
YOU WILL BE IMP

GOD

ATTN: T. SLAGWORTHY

FRIDAY
10.23 A.M.

WHAT THE DEVIL IS GOING ON?   MY SECRETARY HAS JUST RETURNED
FROM SITE IN STATE OF SHOCK. SAYS THE WHOLE SHAMBLES IS
LOOKING WORSE THAN EVER! NOTHING COMPLETE! LAZY WORKMEN!
LAND STILL IN WRONG PLACE! INSECTS ALL FLOWN AWAY! HERBS
HAVE LEAF MOULD!

TELEX YOUR IMMEDIATE REPLY.

GOD

ATTN: T.G. COHEN-COHEN

FRIDAY
12.05 P.M.

THANKS FOR LATEST LETTER. NOTE YOU ARE PLANNING TO
POP OVER TO SITE, BUT SUGGEST IT MIGHT PERHAPS BE
BETTER NOT TO RIGHT NOW. MIGHT UPSET BUILDERS A
BIT. THESE CREATIVE CHAPS CAN BE A BIT TEMPERAMENTAL.

HOW ABOUT TOMORROW AFTERNOON INSTEAD?

(NOTHING TO WORRY ABOUT ... WORLD LOOKING REALLY

FANTASTIC.)

KIND REGARDS.

GOD

ATTN: T. SLAGWORTHY

FRIDAY
12.10 P.M.

WHAT'S GOING ON??
STILL NOT HEARD A THING FROM YOU AND, TO MAKE
MATTERS WORSE, AMALWORLDS ARE NOW ON MY BACK.

GET YOUR FINGER OUT.

GOD

ATTN: T.G. COHEN-COHEN

FRIDAY
2.05 P.M.

HAVE JUST RECEIVED YOUR TELEPHONE MESSAGE. REGRET
I AM UNABLE TO MEET YOU OVER AT THE WORLD FOR A
DRINK THIS EVENING. ANYWAY, THE PUB THERE HAS
A FEW FINAL TOUCHES TO BE ADDED AND THE BEER HASN'T
HAD TIME TO SETTLE. SUGGEST YOU GO HOME AND RELAX
INSTEAD. BESIDES, HAVE JUST HEARD THERE'S VERY,
VERY THICK FOG OVER WORLD AT MOMENT (BUILDERS
TRYING OUT NEW FOG MACHINE). AND IT WILL BE
DARK SOON, SO YOU WON'T SEE ANYTHING ANYWAY.

SUGGEST WE GO TOMORROW OR THEREABOUTS. BETTER
TO WAIT UNTIL ALL WORK ABSOLUTELY COMPLETE SO YOU CAN
REALLY GET THE FEEL OF THE PLACE. WILL CONTACT
TOMORROW TO FIX CONVENIENT TIME.

KIND REGARDS.

GOD

123498 CONU G
112 GOD G

ATTN: SLAGWORTHY

FRIDAY
2.55 P.M.

REPLY OR ELSE.

GOD

ATTN: TED SLAGWORTHY

FRIDAY
3.32 P.M.

RECEIVED YOUR PHONE MESSAGE. NO! WON'T WAIT TILL MONDAY!
IMPERATIVE THAT CREATION OF WHOLE WORLD BE COMPLETE BY
TOMORROW EVENING.

INCIDENTALLY, DON'T BELIEVE FOR A MOMENT THAT YOUR POOR
OLD MOTHER IS CALLING FOR YOU FROM HOSPITAL BED. IN
FACT, DON'T BELIEVE A SINGLE WORD YOU SAY. SKIP THE
EXCUSES.

COMPLETE BY TOMORROW!

GOD

234987 AMALWORLD
112 GOD G
0001/AB

ATTN: T.G. CO

FRIDAY
4.40 P.M.

SO GLAD TO HEAR YOU'VE DECIDED NOT TO VISIT WORLD
THIS EVENING AFTER ALL. AM SURE DECISION IS FOR
THE BEST.

GOD

```
234987 AMALWORLDS G
112 GOD G
0001/AB


    ATTN: T.G. COHEN-COHEN

    SATURDAY


        REGRET NO PROSPECT OF WORLD BEING COMPLETE TODAY
        AFTER ALL.  NOR TOMORROW.
        SORRY.


        GOD


            112 GOD G
        234987 AMALWORLDS G
```

<u>Veronica</u>

Please order an immediate inquiry into the events of last week. Please ask me for details of how the inquiry should be presented. ~~Also~~ Also ask me for details of who the inquiry involves. And what form the inquiry should ~~take~~. Also ask me about anything else you're not more about. In fact, you'd better ask me to arrange everything. Gone to chemist to pick up nerve pills.

G.

"God"

CREATIVE CONSULTANCY PROPERTY SERVICING
Agent for: AMALGAMATED WORLDS Pty.

Registered Office: UNIT 4, LEVEL 2, CENTRAL PLAZA
Telephone: 353 500000 Telex: GOD
Directors: GOD (Managing, Sales, Financial)

Dear Mr. Slagworthy,

Re: Creation of The World

I cannot trust myself to write this letter sanely, so
great is my anger!

Last week an utterly shambolic series of events took
place as a result of the work carried out (or not)
in the name of your company. I hold you personally
responsible. I have ordered a formal inquiry into
the full details, but from my limited inquiries it
would appear you took the very least possible care
and effort in all aspects of the work.

I now have to face the embarrassing and thoroughly
unappetising prospect of a grilling from Amalgamated
Worlds, for which I am sure to pay heavily. This
creation was supposed to be an unforgettable event;
an event that would be written about and talked
of for centuries. Instead, it has proved to be
totally forgettable. Mainly because nothing actually
happened to remember it by.

I shall be writing to you in more detail later but,
meanwhile, I expect to see you in my office tomorrow
(Tuesday) morning without fail to answer all my
questions in this matter.

Yours frothingly,

Veronica Makepiece

pp. God

G.

Mr. Cohen-Cohen phoned while
you were at the psychoanalyst's
V. difficult to hear what he said —
earpiece too hot to put near ear.
Not V. coherent, either!
Seemed V. V. angry.
Said you were to call him the minute
you put so much as a toe though
the door. Said something else about
fingernails being torn out. Also
gave a fairly graphic description
of what happened to people who let
him down (attached. Sorry — pen ran
out after 16 pages).

Think you should phone him. Dont
think I can stand much more!

Veronica

Phone Message : God.

Man from the Hillock Department of Mountain Supply shop rang while you were at the clinic having your face lift. Said he'd got 6 small mountains we'd ordered from him five months ago and could we come round and collect them as they were blocking the goods entrance.

Told him we hadn't bought six hillocks from him. He went away to check, came back and said we were quite right, it was only half a dozen. Called himself a silly hillock and rang off.

Veronica

Telephone Message

TIME RECEIVED _____ DATE _____

FROM _____

GOD MR. (SOUNDED LIKE 'R. MEBLOODY - LEGG) PHONED. SOUNDED VERY AGITATED. SAID WE ORDERED 75,000 'BEASTS THAT MOVETH' FROM HIM SOME WHILE AGO AND DID WE STILL WANT THEM? SAID THEY WERE CLUTTERING UP HIS WAREHOUSE AND MAKING HIS LIFE HELL (ALSO MAKING HIS LIFE DANGEROUS). ASKED IF WE COULD PHONE HIM BACK - BUT BEFORE HE COULD REPLY THERE WAS A ~~SERIOUS~~ STRANGE SORT OF THROTTLED SCREAM AND THE LINE WENT DEAD. VERONICA

RECEIVED BY _____ God.

A. Mr. McSpreader phoned about the 875,000 tons of raw sewage we ordered from him (said we'd told him it was for somewhere called 'Argentina').
Asked if we were still requiring order?
If not, could we please send him a shovel (apparently he lost his last one when the stuff was delivered to him and can't carry on using his hands as all ~~his~~ his fingernails are broken).

Veronica

"god"

CREATIVE CONSULTANCY PROPERTY SERVICING
Agent for: AMALGAMATED WORLDS Pty.

Registered Office: UNIT 4, LEVEL 2, CENTRAL PLAZA
Telephone: 353 500000 Telex: GOD
Directors: GOD (Managing, Sales, Financial)

Dear God,

It is with regret that we, the undersigned, write to inform you that we wish to tender our resignation to take effect as from today.

We regret that we can no longer tolerate the work or the atmosphere in the office and wish to leave before it is too late. This was once a happy, pleasant office with happy staff and pleasant work. However, the work and effort put into the creation of the World has turned this place into a madhouse and we do not feel able to remain here a moment longer.

Already a number of we green elephants have had to receive treatment for mild depression and psychiatric help help an old frying pan is attacking me on the walls pork sausages most frequently thank you and I know I write for all the undersigned when I say, I say that's a nice ostrich feather Mr O'Hennessy but no thank you I've already seen the doctor.

Regretfully yours with thigh bucket stuck on head tomorrow,

Janice	Keith	John	Norman
Winston	Tony	Mark	Denise
Vince	Eamonn	Luke	Elvis
Harriet	Gary	Matthew	The office cat

very, very
STERN & FOREBODING
good solicitors

Dear God,

Re: Creation of The World

We act as solicitors for Amalgamated Worlds and it has been suggested that we write to you in connection with the above matter.

Our clients are becoming alarmed at the delay in completion of this long-overdue project and have asked that as solicitors we look into the possible legal aspects and report them to you.

From our understanding of the situation it would appear that your position is a far from happy one. For you to produce rational and credible justifications for your present plight would, we feel, be about as useful as (to quote an old legal phrase) 'a fart in the wind'. Especially so since we would no doubt be acting against you in court and, though I say so myself, we are a remarkably good firm of solicitors.

In fact we would, with due modesty, place our standing alongside the very best in the legal profession. For instance, in a recent case, Prosecuting Counsel was heard to say, "This is an open and shut case if ever I saw one. The lad is guilty and no amount of fancy talk will get him off." Yet not only was the lad let off scot-free, but he also got substantial damages in the process. Naturally, the Defence as presented by yours truly was the only thing that got him off. Being the magistrate's son must have helped him a bit, too, but I do think that, without .... his case would have been lost. But I digress.

Page 1

POSTCARD

AFFIX
STAMP
HERE

DEAR GOD,
WEATHER FINE! FOOD
GREAT! WILD NIGHTLIFE!
WISH YOU WERE HERE.
HAVE DECIDED TO SPEND
~~A FEW DAYS~~ ~~A WEEK~~ A
FORTNIGHT OR SO HERE
AT THE SEASIDE.
P.S. FORGOT TO SWITCH OFF
WATER WHEN WE LEFT.
PSE DO US V. BIG FAVOUR
- NIP OVER THERE AND
SWITCH IT OFF. STOPCOCK
IS SOMEWHERE UNDER
NORTH AFRICA.
COSMIC AND
UNIVERSAL

NAME   GOD
ADDRESS UNIT 4
         LEVEL 2
         CENTRAL PLAZA.

The view shows the attractive Solarium and Massage Parlour shortly before a raid by Vice Squad detectives.

254.
0001/AB

ATTN: GOD

MOST, MOST URGENT! WHAT IN THE WORLD IS GOING ON.
EXPECTED ALL WORK TO BE COMPLETED BY NOW. MOST
ANXIOUS THAT THIS BE DONE BY NINE O'CLOCK MONDAY
MORNING WITHOUT FAIL OR I'LL BE ROUND TO GIVE YOU
WHAT-FOR PERSONALLY.

MOST = REPEAT MOST = URGENT

T.G. COHEN-COHEN

---

young villain would surely have swung from the gallows, and no mistake! So take heed. Any fancy business and I'll have you in the nick faster than you can say 'Old Bailey!'

Yours legally and bindingly,

J P Primp

J. P. Primp, Q.C.
For Stern and Foreboding

Page 17

CREATIVE CONSULTANCY PROPERTY SERVICING
Agent for: AMALGAMATED WORLDS Pty.

Registered Office: UNIT 4, LEVEL 2, CENTRAL PLAZA
Telephone: 353 500000 Telex: GOD
Directors: GOD (Managing, Sales, Financial)

Dear Mr. Slagworthy,

Re: Creation Of The World

Thank you for your letter and invoice, both of which I
have thrown straight into the wastepaper-bin. I am
quite unable to recall another occasion on which I
have been so angry though, goodness knows, during the
course of this project there have been plenty of
opportunities.

Not only do I consider your request for payment an
impudent act of bravado following your appalling record
to date, but I also consider the request for the full
amount quite outrageous in view of the fact that you
have barely completed the first quarter of the work
required. In all my years in business I have never
been so incensed. You ruin my personal and professional
standing in the community, then seek payment for the
privilege!

You are, Sir, with respect, a despicable con-man and your
so-called company is a total disgrace. I bitterly regret
the day I ever allowed myself to consider you for this
most prestigious of projects, and you may be quite certain
that I will never again make the same mistake.

You may be equally certain that your invoice will not be
paid in 30 days as you request. Nor in 60 days. Nor in
180 days. In fact, I doubt that if you lived to be 150
you would see it paid! I suggest that if you want so
much as to smell even a penny of the settlement you will
(a) show that you are willing to complete the work in
hand diligently, responsibly and thoroughly; and (b)
phone or call to convey such an intention at the earliest
opportunity.

Until such time, I do not wish to see or hear from y
company again.

Yours disgustedly,

Veronica Makepiece

PP. God

Telephone Message

TIME RECEIVED __10·45__   DATE _____

FROM __Mr. SLAGWORTHY__

GOD

MR. SLAGWORTHY PHONED. SAID 'HOW
ABOUT TUESDAY?' — TOLD HIM I WAS
BUSY. HE SAID 'NO, HOW ABOUT TUESDAY
FOR THE MEETING?' SAID WE WOULD
CONFIRM.

RECEIVED BY *Veronica*

CREATIVE CONSULTANCY PROPERTY SERVICING
Agent for: AMALGAMATED WORLDS Pty.
Registered Office: UNIT 4, LEVEL 2, CENTRAL PLAZA
Telephone: 353 500000 Telex: GOD
Directors: GOD (Managing, Sales, Financial)

Dear Mr. Slagworthy,

Re: Creation Of The World

I look forward to seeing you at 9.00 very, very sharp
in my office on Tuesday morning.

Be punctual.

Yours briefly,

Veronica Makepiece

PP. God

Minutes of Meeting Held 9.00 a.m. Tuesday to Discuss

THE CREATION OF THE WORLD

Those present: God

Mr. Slagworthy (Cosmic & Universal Construction Co.)

The following points were raised:

1. God called Mr. Slagworthy a ████████ !
2. God also called Mr. Slagworthy a ████████ ████████ !
3. God intimated that Mr. Slagworthy could ████████ ████████ ████ !
4. God paused for breath
5. Mr. Slagworthy apologised
6. God said apologies weren't enough
7. Mr. Slagworthy grovelled on his knees and apologised profusely
8. God said all right, all right he accepted the apologies
9. Mr. Slagworthy said good, how about some money?
10. God called Mr. Slagworthy an ████████ ███ ████████ !
11. Mr. Slagworthy said thank you
12. God said when could work be expected to start again?
13. Mr. Slagworthy said he must be leaving
14. God said when could work be expected to start again?
15. Mr. Slagworthy put on his hat and coat
16. God tied Mr. Slagworthy to a chair with a piece of string
17. God said now, when could work be expected to start again?
18. Mr. Slagworthy said stop, stop, you're hurting me
19. Mr. Slagworthy said two weeks on Friday
20. Mr. Slagworthy said stop, stop, I can't breathe
21. Mr. Slagworthy said next Thursday
22. God said this was hurting him more than it was hurting Mr. Slagworthy
23. Mr. Slagworthy said tomorrow
24. God tightened the thumbscrews
25. Mr. Slagworthy promised tomorrow and said he'd put it in writing
26. God passed him a pen and a piece of paper
27. Mr. Slagworthy said he didn't know how to write
28. God taught him
29. Mr. Slagworthy mentioned the word reluctance a lot
30. God mentioned the word violence a lot
31. God and Mr. Slagworthy shook hands
MEETING CLOSED

234987 AMALWORLDS G
112 GOD G

ATTN: T.G. COHEN-COHEN

VERY CORDIAL MEETING TODAY BETWEEN SELF AND BUILDER.
AMICABLY AGREED THAT WORK ON CREATION WOULD START
TOMORROW (WEDNESDAY) AND BE FINISHED WITHIN FIVE
DAYS WITHOUT FAIL.

GOD

```
234987 AMALWORLDS G
112 GOD G
0001/AB


        ATTN: T.G. COHEN-COHEN

        HAVE INSTALLED PERMANENT OVERSEER AT SITE TO
        REPORT ON PROGRESS.  BY ALL ACCOUNTS ALL GOING VERY
        WELL.  BUILDERS PRESENT.  HAVE STARTED TO PUMP
        OUT SLIME AND CLEAR SITE.  HAVE ALSO MANAGED TO
        INSTALL A LIMITED SOURCE OF LIGHT AND DARKNESS.
        FIRST TESTS OF EVERY THING THAT CREEPETH DUE TO
        START THIS AFTERNOON.  HERB YIELDING SEED NOW
        PLANTED AND PROVING SUCCESSFUL.

        SLIGHT PROBLEM WITH GREAT WHALES BUT HAVE ORDERED
        HALF-A-DOZEN MORE.  ALSO ICE CAPS KEEP SLIPPING
        AND HAVE HAD TO BE SCREWED DOWN IN PLACE FOR
        TIME BEING.

        OTHER THAN THESE TEETHING TROUBLES, EVERYTHING
        GOING WELL.  DELIGHTED THEREFORE TO BE ABLE TO
        REPORT PROGRESS ON SCHEDULE! TRUST THIS WILL GIVE
        YOU AS MUCH SATISFACTION AS IT DID ME.


        REGARDS.


        GOD
```

Telephone Message

TIME RECEIVED 12.30 DATE _____

FROM OVERSEER

OVERSEER PHONED WHILE YOU WERE OUT
AT THE COBBLER'S. REPORTS PROGRESS STILL
GOING REASONABLY WELL, BUT SLIGHT
PROBLEM WITH FISH. GILLS APPARENTLY
FAULTY. SO FAR 20,000 DEAD, BUT HAVE
MANAGED TO HIDE THEM ALL UNDER
BELGIUM. SLIGHT SMELL, BUT THINKS IT
WILL DIE AWAY.

RECEIVED BY VERONICA

Telephone Message

TIME RECEIVED 2.30 DATE _____

FROM OVERSEER

GOD

OVERSEER PHONED TO REPORT PROGRESS
GOING 'REASONABLY'. LIGHT AND DARKNESS
NOW SPLIT. HINGES PUT ON ITALY. NEW
COASTLINES FITTED TO SWITZERLAND. STILL
PROBLEM WITH BELGIUM (BEGINNING TO
SMELL QUITE CONSIDERABLY)

CEIVED BY VERONICA

Telephone Message

TIME RECEIVED 3.40 DATE _____

FROM OVERSEER

OVERSEER CALLED TO SAY WORK
'STILL PROGRESSING'. LIGHT AND DARKNESS
FAILED (TWICE). BELGIUM SMELLING
ABOMINABLY AND HAS TO BE TOWED INTO
MIDDLE OF ATLANTIC OCEAN. ICELAND
FITTED WRONG WAY ROUND BUT TOO LATE
TO DO ANYTHING ABOUT IT.

RECEIVED BY VERONICA

... RECEIVED 4.20 DATE _____

FROM OVERSEER

HAVING PROBLEMS WITH NORTH AMERICA.
WON'T FIT. MIGHT HAVE TO SAW OFF
IRELAND AND PUT IT SOMEWHERE ELSE.
NORWAY HAS GOT SOME RATHER NASTY
SCORCH MARKS AS A RESULT OF A FIRE.
WILL REPORT AGAIN TOMORROW.

VERONICA.

RECEIVED BY _____

Thursday

Dear God,

Following the telephone calls I made to your office yesterday
about the slight hitches here at The World site, I am pleased
to report that reasonable progress is once again being made.
Some of the countries are now complete and several more aren't
far off. In addition, seed from the seed bearing fruit have
been brought forth, and there are abundant living creatures that
moveth. In fact, there are more than abundant living creatures
that moveth, which is why progress hasn't been as fast as we'd
hoped in some other areas.

For instance, the climates have proved somewhat problematical,
since they were located in different places to those which
appeared on the specifications. (At the moment the Equator
is in the grips of Arctic blizzards, while Europe is enjoying
the monsoon season.)

In addition, there have been not inconsiderable problems with
the gravity mechanism for holding items onto The World's
surface. It is certainly not complying with the specifications,
and animals, trees and even small hills are apt to spin off
at great speeds.

However, that Slagworthy man rolled up in his XJS this morning
and said that he knows of a firm that can supply a very
strong rubber-based adhesive especially for this purpose.
Nevertheless, it will take a while for matters to be put to
rights, especially as all the items that dropped off have yet
to be retrieved.

Yours creepily,

Uriah Snooper.

Uriah Snooper
Overseer

"God"

CREATIVE CONSULTANCY PROPERTY SERVICING
Agent for: AMALGAMATED WORLDS Pty.
Registered Office: UNIT 4, LEVEL 2, CENTRAL PLAZA
Telephone: 353 500000 Telex: GOD
Directors: GOD (Managing, Sales, Financial)

Friday

Dear Mr. Cohen-Cohen,

Re: Creation of The World

I have just had a letter and urgent phone call from my over-seer at The World site who has informed me that, while very reasonable progress is being made, there are still a few snags to be ironed out which in turn may leave us somewhat stretched to meet Sunday's deadline.

I believe I mentioned to you the problem with the gravity mechanism and it does seem that this has become rather more serious than when I last wrote. In particular, a number of continents have worked loose and have started to bump into one another in a slightly dangerous manner. Luckily, the builders were able to rope most of them down before any really serious damage was caused but it does mean that other work has been unavoidably delayed.

Yours apologetically,

Veronica Makepiece

PP. God

ATTN: GOD

IN RECEIPT OF YOUR LETTER. CONTENTS NOT AT ALL WELL RECEIVED HERE AT AMALWORLDS. PLS OBTAIN IMMEDIATELY A REALISTIC INDICATION AS TO WHEN WORLD LIKELY TO BE COMPLETED. TELEX DETAILS AT ONCE.

T.G. COHEN-COHEN

Telephone Message

TIME RECEIVED _3.30._ DATE _____

FROM _Cos. + Univ. Const. Co._

GOD:

MR. SLAGWORTHY PHONED WHILE YOU WERE OUT AT THE CAR AUCTION. SAID THAT GRAVITY PROBLEM WAS MUCH WORSE THAN AT FIRST ANTICIPATED, AND WAS NOT OPTIMISTIC ABOUT FINISHING WORK IN UNDER 2 YEARS. (ONE PIECE OF GOOD NEWS — THE PROBLEM WITH THE LIZARDS HAS BEEN SOLVED)

RECEIVED BY _____   *VERONICA*

123498 CONU G
112 GOD G

ATTN: TED SLAGWORTHY

MUST RETHINK! TWO YEARS PURE FANTASY. SUGGEST MEETING TOMORROW TO DISCUSS SOLUTION.

GOD

112 GOD G
123498 CONU G

CREATIVE CONSULTANCY PROPERTY SERVICING
Agent for: AMALGAMATED WORLDS Pty.

Registered Office: UNIT 4, LEVEL 2, CENTRAL PLAZA
Telephone: 353 500000 Telex: GOD
Directors: GOD (Managing, Sales, Financial)

CREATION OF THE WORLD

OFFICIAL transcript of meeting between God and Cosmic &
Universal Construction Co. to discuss further progress
on the above project.

1.   It was reported that the problems with the gravity mechanism were
     in fact far more serious than at first anticipated and could not
     be resolved with the materials available.

2.   It was suggested that if the world was to revolve at a much slower
     speed things might not fly off quite so readily. However, it was
     pointed out that if the world revolved at a slower speed it would
     be liable to upset the delicate light-darkness mechanism and lead
     to it being pitch black at lunchtime and bright and clear at midnight.

3.   It was suggested that if continents could be nailed down the gravity
     problem might be overcome. However, it was also suggested that
     this solution could not be applied to the creeping things that
     creepeth, or to the fish that swimmeth, or the winged fowl that
     flyeth, all of whom would prove very difficult to nail down. However,
     it was agreed to sanction fish experiments to see if fish could not be
     nailed to the ground without causing undue stress or suffering.
     Mr. Slagworthy said he knew of a firm who specialised in just such
     work and would contact them to see if they would be willing to carry
     out the experiments.

4.   It was also pointed out that several other problems had arisen that
     could not have been anticipated. It was reported that the plastic
     grass was not suitable for grazing animals since the beasts were
     showing a tendency to become very thin and die of starvation.

5.   It was pointed out to the builders that the one bag of sand as
     listed in the specifications was insufficient to cover the large
     amount of desert-land required, and it was agreed that Cosmic &
     Universal Construction should provide at no extra cost another half-
     dozen bags to complete the work.

6.   It was agreed that the magnetic-type fixing used on certain continents
     (namely New Zealand, Japan and Edinburgh) was unnecessarily
     complicated and should be discarded immediately.

7.   It was agreed that the installation of man was now a matter of some
     urgency.

8.   It was agreed that a new schedule should be prepared.

COSMIC & UNIVERSAL CONSTRUCTION CO.
General Builders & Contractors

3rd Arch Along
Limepit Viaduct
Telephone 18194804612 (one line)
Telex CONU

MEMBER OF THE FEDERATION OF SMALL BUILDERS
AND BUILDING CONTRACTORS

S C H E D U L E

Week 1	Clear site. Repair surface using Fix-i-Bond High-impact Ocean and Continent Adhesive.
Week 2	Apply second coat of Fix-i-Bond. Apply Sealer. Apply Primer. Apply heavy weights and leave for 24 hours in the airing cupboard.
Week 3	Scour site. Affix continents in position using $\frac{1}{2}$ in. carpet tacks at 6 in. intervals.
Week 4	Using staple gun, staple all shorelines into position. Staple all coastal erosive features into position. Using Gum-It! Multi-purpose Fixative, affix all cliffs and headlands firmly in place.
Week 5	Using KEEP-U-DRY Coastline Tape, seal all coastlines and shores to ensure watertight bond. Treat continents with Thermo-warm Continental Primer. Apply undercoat. Sand and seal.
Week 6	Using a spirit level, ensure all working surfaces are level. Conduct gravity tests with world spinning at half speed.
Week 7	Overhaul and re-assemble light and darkness. Switch on and test.
Week 8	Overhaul climate. Switch on and test. Install camels. Install manure. Apply manure to herbs and seeds.
Week 9	Assemble beasts that creepeth, fish that swimmeth, winged fowl that flyeth.
Week 10	Road test beasts that creepeth, fish that swimmeth, winged fowl that flyeth.
Week 11	Assemble and install man and woman.
Week 12	Road test man and woman.
Week 13	G.B.A.

TOTAL 13 WEEKS : 3 MONTHS

234987 AMALWORLDS G
112 GOD G
0001/AB

ATTN: T.G. COHEN-COHEN

HAD MEETING WITH SLAGWORTHY (BUILDER). SUGGESTED
TIME SCALE NOW 13 WEEKS MAXIMUM.

OFFICIAL.

WILL FORWARD DETAILS.

REGARDS

GOD

112 GOD G
234987 AMALWORLDS G

123498 CONU G
112 GOD G

ATTN: GOD

HAVE BEGUN (AGAIN). TRIED TO SOLVE GRAVITY PROBLEMS.
IMMEDIATE SNAG. WORLD WILL NOT REVOLVE NOW.
MECHANISM SEIZED UP. TRIED TO FREE IT WITH MECHANICAL
DIGGER. DIGGER RUINED. WORLD NOW TILTED TO ONE SIDE.
NOW RESTING ON TWO BRICKS AND BLOCK OF WOOD.

    PLEASE ADVISE.

    TED SLAGWORTHY

    123498 CONU G
    112 GOD G

123498 CONU G
112 GOD G

ATTN: GOD

GOOD NEWS — WORLD NOW REVOLVING AGAIN. BAD NEWS —
NOW REVOLVING IN REVERSE. DEVASTATING EFFECT. ALL
VEGETATION RIPPED OFF. BIRDS FLYING BACKWARDS.
INSECTS IN STATE OF DEEP SHOCK.
WIRING ON CLIMATES BURNT OUT. SNOW FALLING ALTHOUGH
TEMPERATURE OVER 105° F. HEAT HAS CAUSED CONTINENTS
TO COME UNSTUCK. FIX-I-BOND GLUE EVERYWHERE. ANIMALS
STUCK TO CONTINENTS.

    SITUATION NOT PROMISING.

    TED SLAGWORTHY
    (MR SLAGWORTHY, I'M STUCK TO THE TELEX MACHINE. HELP.
    GWYN)

    123498 CONU G
    112 GOD G

God

    Surveyor phoned to report on
state of creation. Sounded V. distraught
Said he was a surveyor, not a
magician! Said he was returning
our fee as he was unable to complete
the work under any circumstances.
Asked if I should get you to contact
him but he just started to cry and
    hung up.   Veronica

---

112 GOD G
234987 AMALWORLDS G
0001/AB

ATTN: GOD

WHAT IS HAPPENING? YOU'VE BEEN REMARKABLY
QUIET OF LATE. REPORT AT ONCE. AM UNDER
ENORMOUS PRESSURE FROM MANAGING DIRECTOR.

    T.G. COHEN-COHEN

    234987 AMAL
    112 GOD G

CREATIVE CONSULTANCY PROPERTY SERVICING
Agent for: AMALGAMATED WORLDS Pty.
Registered Office: UNIT 4, LEVEL 2, CENTRAL PLAZA
Telephone: 353 500000 Telex: GOD
Directors: GOD (Managing, Sales, Financial)

Dear Mr. Cohen-Cohen,

Re: Creation Of The World

I am very much aware of the burden which has been thrust upon
you as a result of the further delay in completing the above
project. I understand that one or two mechanical problems are
responsible for the hold-up and I shall, of course, be submitting
more details about these as soon as I have a clearer reading
of the situation.

In the meantime, I thought you might like to see the brochure
and 'Scratch 'n' Sniff' card we have had prepared for the
launch of the project. I'm sure you'll agree they are most
impressive, and trust they might compensate for the unfortunately
long wait.

Yours evasively,

Veronica Makepiece

PP God

Enclosures

A BRAND NEW WORLD!

A world created for you ... your children ... and your children's children. A world planned in meticulous detail because we believe that, if a world is worth creating at all, it's worth creating well. So you can be sure it will work — day in, day out. It's a world you will be proud of. A world you'll never want to leave. Because it's YOUR world.

Features include: 'Rock effect' on all mountain faces/intertropical convergence zone/edible wildlife/Salopian outwash fans/tight T-shirts/Malaysia/marshland scenery/geysers/fault line scarps/Bolton/transfluent laterite soils/squally showers/quicksand/proluval stratigraphy/Glasgow/tors/

INCLUDES Thermal cladding; insulation; fail-safe device; dead man's handle; auxiliary brakes; automatic cut-out; electrical valves; self-lubricating axis; thermostatic control; ceramic chip-proof finish; posture springing; lumbar support.

SPECIAL CHARACTERISTICS

Man and Woman • Integral hills • Wet water • Non-combustible wildlife • Full range of climates • Diverse trees • Wide selection of plants • Unique smell • Automatic night and day • Choice of countries • Beasts that creepeth • Vegetation that doesn't creepeth all that much.

nubile 16-year old schoolgirls/truncated spurs/isothermic gradients/peek-a-boo bras/trade winds/Hull/barrier reefs/fenland/graded sediment/prairies/loam/France/ready-made fossils/firm young bosoms thrusting against see-through negligées/selva/tornadoes/Germany (x2)/monoliths/Cyprus/clinographic curves.

SPAIN!•

As a special bonus with this — and only this — world, we are supplying you with a free Spain for you to install and use however you see fit (machine gun and rifles not included).
• or cash equivalent.

NO ARTIFICIAL INGREDIENTS

We have used no artificial ingredients in preparing this world. Not many, anyway. Well, certainly not all that many we're prepared to tell you about.

IT'S OUR WORLD

We have built this world large enough so there's space for everyone. Space to breathe. Space to spread. Space to do anything else you had in mind*. You'll never feel cramped, no matter how large your requirements. Which is why you'll never mind saying 'It's Our World'.
* see doctor for full details.

OWN MAN AND WOMAN!!

The world comes complete with ready-made, fully assembled man and woman (batteries not included). Made to highest specifications imaginable. Each man and woman outfit includes spare ear, spare leg, spare teeth and spare femero-cutaneous nerve.

OFFICIAL
SCRATCH 'N' SNIFF CARD

Enjoy the smells of the new World
IN THE COMFORT OF YOUR OWN HOME!

Simply scratch* then sniff to enjoy the smell of:

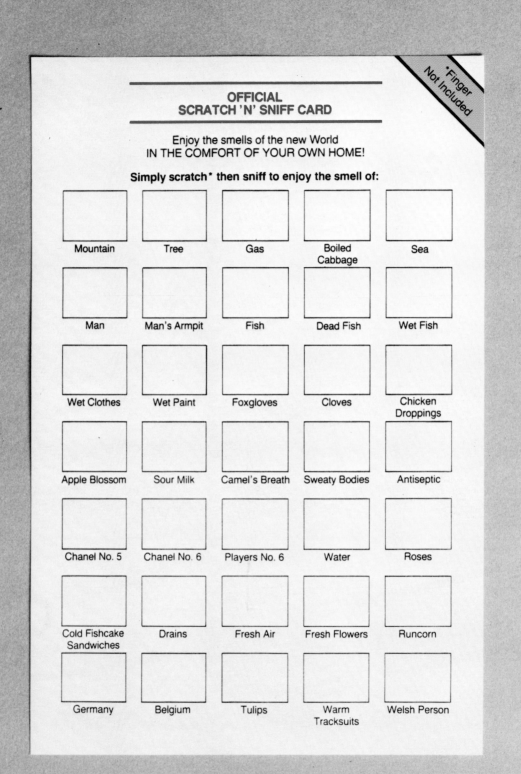

Mountain	Tree	Gas	Boiled Cabbage	Sea
Man	Man's Armpit	Fish	Dead Fish	Wet Fish
Wet Clothes	Wet Paint	Foxgloves	Cloves	Chicken Droppings
Apple Blossom	Sour Milk	Camel's Breath	Sweaty Bodies	Antiseptic
Chanel No. 5	Chanel No. 6	Players No. 6	Water	Roses
Cold Fishcake Sandwiches	Drains	Fresh Air	Fresh Flowers	Runcorn
Germany	Belgium	Tulips	Warm Tracksuits	Welsh Person

112 GOD G

ATTN: GOD

GLAD TO REPORT PROGRESS. SEAS NOW UNPACKED AND IN FULL
WORKING ORDER. HOLLYHOCKS = SORRY, HILLOCKS = NOW
INSTALLED AND LOOKING GOOD.

HOWEVER, SOMEONE LEFT MONSOON CLIMATE ON OVERNIGHT AND
MUCH OF ASIA DAMAGED. HUNG ON LINE TO DRY. PLEASE
CONFIRM WE CAN CLAIM ON INSURANCE.

ANTELOPE YOU SUPPLIED FAULTY ... KEEPS TRYING TO BREED
WITH MONKEYS. TREES A BIT SMALL ... KEEP TRIPPING OVER
THEM.

OTHERWISE OK.

TED SLAGWORTHY

123498 CONU G

---

112 GOD G

ATTN: GOD

NEVER MIND THE BROCHURE AND THAT SMELLY THING, HOW'S
THE WORK PROGRESSING? DEMAND YOU GET IN TOUCH
IMMEDIATELY TO ADVISE.

COHEN-COHEN

---

112 GOD G

ATTN: GOD

REGRET TO REPORT NUMBER OF MISHAPS. DUE TO
UNFORTUNATE TYPING ERROR ON ORDER FORM, HAVE
JUST TAKEN DELIVERY OF BREASTS THAT CREEPETH.

NUMBER OF ELEPHANTS KILLED. SUGGEST WE REMOVE
WINGS, OR AT LEAST CLIP THEM.

95 FEET OF SNOW IN COLORADO. IS THIS RIGHT (NOT
ON SPECIFICATIONS)? SUGGEST YOU SUPPLY SHOVEL
AND SNOWPLOUGH.

HOLDING YOU RESPONSIBLE FOR ACCIDENTS/FAULTS/
DELAYS. YOU OBVIOUSLY WOULDN'T RECOGNISE A
COMPETENT SUPPLIER IF ONE CAME UP AND KICKED
YOU ON THE SHIN.

TED SLAGWORT

123498 CONU G

---

112 GOD G

ATTN: GOD

OUR REPORTS SHOW INSPECTOR'S PROCEDURES OVERLOOKED/
INATTENTION TO DETAIL/INSUFFICIENT CARE AND CONTROL/
MISMANAGEMENT/MALADMINISTRATION.

ALSO, CHART SHOWS WORK FALLING BEHIND ON ALL SCHEDULES.

REPORT NOW.

T.G. COHEN-COHEN

234987 AMALWORLDS G

</>

CREATIVE CONSULTANCY PROPERTY SERVICING
Agent for: AMALGAMATED WORLDS Pty.
Registered Office: UNIT 4, LEVEL 2, CENTRAL PLAZA
Telephone: 353 500000 Telex: GOD
Directors: GOD (Managing, Sales, Financial)

Dear Mr. Cohen-Cohen,

Re: Creation Of The World

I have spoken to Mr. God today who has asked that I contact
you in connection with a number of letters to which you have
not, I believe, received any reply.

Unfortunately, Mr. God has been away from the office for some
time with a serious illness brought on by overwork and
exhaustion. His doctor has not apparently been able to
diagnose the illness from symptoms listed in any of the
standard medical textbooks, though I believe he did find
reference to it in a back copy of 'Know Your Gerbils'.
However, I understand Mr. God is now recovering well and
should shortly be allowed out of the asylum. We trust, therefore,
that he will be back in the office within the next few
weeks.

He has in the meantime asked that I convey to you the
situation as he was concerned lest you should worry. I
know he has an extremely large pile of correspondence awaiting his return but he assured me (through the oxygen tent)
that yours would be the first matter to which he would
address himself upon his return.

Meanwhile, I enclose herewith a copy of the me
for your files.

Yours sincerely,

Veronica Makepiece

Veronica Makepiece
Personal Assistant to Mr. God

Enclosure

Patient's Name	MEDICAL REPORT
N. I. No.	God
Symptoms	ZZ 4563874855

psychosis, nausea, vomiting, lack of appetite, tiredness,
migraines, loss of smell, loss of memory (leading to lo
of bicycle), severe itching, severe coughing, chestiness
chest pains, burning sensation in back of throat, burning
sensation in back of mouth, burning sensation in back
pocket of trousers (leading to inflammation of the trouser
inflammation of the hair, inability to stand up properly,
inability to stand around, inability to stand a round,
Scottish accent, earache, hysteria, throbbing in the lower
abdominal cavity, throbbing in the lower shin, throbbing
in the loins, hot and cold flushes, 'feeling not quite right',
stiffness of the right elbow, stiffness of the left nostril',
stiffness of the brain, tingling in the kneecaps, fear of
tadpoles, fear of pumpkins, fear of veal and ham pie, fear
of any type of fresh vegetable, athlete's foot, common cold,

Remedy	
	Rest!

"God"

CREATIVE CONSULTANCY PROPERTY SERVICING

Agent for: AMALGAMATED WORLDS Pty.

Registered Office: UNIT 4, LEVEL 2, CENTRAL PLAZA
Telephone: 353 500000 Telex: GOD
Directors: GOD (Managing, Sales, Financial)

Dear Mr. Cohen-Cohen,

I have only this morning hobbled back to my desk, to
find your request awaiting me. I am therefore supplying
herewith a report on progress of The World project to
date.

Yours painfully,

Veronica Makepiece

pp. God

Enclosure

CREATION OF THE WORLD

Report by the Official Overseer

I would report thus:

The world is ~~not~~ nearly finished. There appears ~~to have been very little~~ *has considerable*
progress since I last inspected the property and indeed in certain instances *but for a few*
~~there even appears to have been a noticeable deterioration.~~ *the world now appears ready to be launched*

I am of the opinion that the work required to complete this project may take *ready tonight*
at ~~least several weeks~~ and could ~~not~~ possibly be considered until a number of *the most two days*

~~major structural works have been completed.~~

It is my opinion that very little work is in fact being undertaken by the *the*
builders at present ~~and it would appear that they have little intention of~~ *is of the highest*
~~involving themselves to any great degree in the foreseeable future.~~ *possible and is a credit to their profession*

I would strongly recommend ~~that in the light of this you consider engaging~~ *early viewing*
~~new workmen to complete the project.~~

Ulrich Snooper.

Overseer

Veronica
Pse amend and retype
as shown. Pass to me
for forgery of the overseer's
signature, then forward
to Amalgamated Worlds
G/

112 GOD G
123498 CONU G

ATTN: GOD

FURTHER TO YOUR REQUEST THAT I VISIT SITE AGAIN,
AM PLEASED AND UTTERLY ASTONISHED TO REPORT
GOOD = REPEAT GOOD = PROGRESS AT LAST BEING
MADE.

THIS IS NOT A HOAX!

WORK WELL ADVANCED. BUILDERS HERE AND WORKING!
NO PROBLEMS THAT I CAN SEE, AND I ESTIMATE WELL
OVER THREE-QUARTERS OF WORK DONE.

FRANKLY AMAZED.

SUGGEST YOU CONFIRM FOR YOURSELF.

URIAH SNOOPER
OVERSEER

"God"

CREATIVE CONSULTANCY PROPERTY SERVICING
Agent for: AMALGAMATED WORLDS Pty.
Registered Office: UNIT 4, LEVEL 2, CENTRAL PLAZA
Telephone: 353 500000 Telex: GOD
Directors: GOD (Managing, Sales, Financial)

Dear Mr. Cohen-Cohen,

Re: Creation Of The World

I am sure you will be delighted and relieved to learn
that at long last real progress is being made on our
project.

My overseer contacted me earlier today with the good
news, whereupon I visited the site this afternoon to
confirm for myself that the man was not hallucinating.
However, the work really is progressing well, and at
a good rate.

Needless to say, I am very relieved and am sure you will
feel equally euphoric. I can hardly believe that within
the not-too-distant future we shall at last be ready.

Yours jubilantly,

Veronica Makepiece

pp. God

P.S.
I have, incidentally, attached a number of photographs
as proof as I know that you may at this juncture be
doubting my sanity.

```
234987 AMALWORLDS G
112 GOD G
0001/AB



   ATTN: T.G. COHEN-COHEN

   WORLD READY BY NOON TOMORROW AT LATEST!
   HAVE CONFIRMED WITH THE BUILDERS, WHO INFORM
   ME THAT JUST ONE DAY'S WORK (ASSEMBLING AND
   ROAD TESTING MAN AND WOMAN) AT MOST.
   TOTALLY OVERWHELMED!
   TRUST YOU WILL JOIN ME IN A TOAST.


      GOD


      112 GOD G
      234987 AMALWORLDS G
```

"GOD"

CREATIVE CONSULTANCY PROPERTY SERVICING
Agent for: AMALGAMATED WORLDS Pty.

Registered Office: UNIT 4, LEVEL 2, CENTRAL PLAZA
Telephone: 353 500000 Telex: GOD
Directors: GOD (Managing, Sales, Financial)

Dear Mr. Cohen-Cohen,

Re: Creation Of The World

I fear I may have unfortunately spoken a trifle too
soon in my last telex. Having cured all the outstanding
technical problems, we were preparing for perhaps the
final day's work, at which point a rather petty squabble
developed between two groups of workers. It is the kind
of thing that happens on building sites all the time, and
it is thankfully the sort of thing that usually cools
down after a few heated exchanges.

Unfortunately, I'm afraid that in this instance there was
little sign of it cooling down, and one of the foremen
was therefore asked to step in. In retrospect, his threat
of immediate dismissal to all concerned might perhaps be
seen as unduly hasty. Certainly that was how the workers
saw it, with the unhappy result that we now find ourselves
with a strike on our hands. Or rather a strike by our
hands.

The dispute originally began, I believe, because those
workers concerned with the assembly of Australia felt
they were not being paid the same rate as those workers
concerned with the assembly of America. Well, to cut
a very long story short, it does appear that we are now
faced with what will doubtless be a protracted dispute
involving management and the two opposing factions.
Management won't speak to the workmen. The workmen won't
speak to management. The workforce is divided and won't
speak to one other. And no one will speak to me.

We have tried all means of reasoning with the workers but
without success. I have personally suggested bribery,
violence, corruption and garrotting. All to no effect.

We are now therefore at an impasse with all work stopped.
I do regret that my earlier jubilation has now had to be
curtailed somewhat, but fear the situation was not one I
could have anticipated.

With much abject regret,

Veronica Makepiece

PP God

AMALGAMATED WORLDS Pty

BIGGEST IN THE UNIVERSE

AMALGAMATED WORLDS PTY
AMALGAMATED WORLDS CORPORATION HOUSE
AMALGAMATED WORLDS CORPORATION PLAZA
AMALGAMATED WORLDS CORPORATION AVENUE
AMALGAMATED WORLDS CORPORATION VILLE

TELEPHONE: 964359214 to 954359792 (inclusive)
TELEX: AMALWORLDS

Dear God,

Re: Creation Of The World

It is with regret that I have to report that Mr. Cohen-Cohen,
with whom I know you have dealt for some considerable time,
was today rushed most unexpectedly to hospital suffering
from what the doctors have diagnosed as chronic hysteria.

I believe Mr. Cohen-Cohen was in the process of reading a
letter from you when the attack took place and I thought it
prudent that you should be made aware of the situation.

I know Mr. Cohen-Cohen wished for me to contact you - indeed,
he talked of little else but you on the journey to the hospital.
In fact you and blunt instruments seemed to be the only thing
he talked about. That was when he spoke. The rest of the
journey he spent gazing up at the roof of the ambulance and
making strange clucking sounds rather like a hen.

In Mr. Cohen-Cohen's absence I shall be dealing with all enquires
and I will be in touch with you again as soon as I have had the
chance to fully acquaint myself with the situation relating to
The World project.

Yours sincerely,

Louis Cheeseberger
Louis Cheeseberger
Project Development Officer (Acting)

"god"

CREATIVE CONSULTANCY PROPERTY SERVICING
Agent for: AMALGAMATED WORLDS Pty.
Registered Office: UNIT 4, LEVEL 2, CENTRAL PLAZA
Telephone: 353 500000 Telex: GOD
Directors: GOD (Managing, Sales, Financial)

Dear Mr. Cheeseberger,

Re: Creation Of The World

Following your request that I put down on paper the points
raised during our heated telephone conversation this morning,
the situation is as follows:

The deadlock has not been broken yet and, if anything, the
position is now even more firmly entrenched.

The workers assembling the vegetation have claimed their
work is more arduous than that of those assembling the pre-
formed volcanos and have demanded that their wages be adjusted
accordingly.

The workers making the beasts that creepeth have stopped work
until they are paid danger money.

The workers making the final adjustments to Asia are claiming
an unsocial hours allowance.

And the workers creating the insects have put in for a new
bonus scheme.

The net result is that everyone appears to be in dispute with
everybody else. I have attached a list of the workers'
additional demands for your reference and we have appealed
to them to return to work pending an enquiry. So far this
request has not been met.

Yours moderately,

Veronica

PP. God

Enclosure

WORKERS' DEMANDS

1. New clocking-on bonus to be introduced for those workers
    bothering to clock on.

2. Clocking-off bonus to be introduced for those workers bothering
    to clock off.

3. New 'serpent bonus' to be paid to all those workers whose work
    brings them into contact with the serpent.

4. Those workers not receiving a serpent bonus to be given a special
    'non-serpent bonus'.

5. New tea-break bonus to be paid to all workers having tea-breaks

6. New afternoon-off bonus to be paid to all workers taking the
    afternoon off.

7. Workers working on Asia to receive an immediate back-dated
    rise for no reason at all.

8. All other workers to receive a similar back-dated pay ri
    bring them into line.

9. Holiday entitlement to be increased from one sabbath a

"God"

CREATIVE CONSULTANCY PROPERTY SERVICING
Agent for: AMALGAMATED WORLDS Pty.

Registered Office: UNIT 4, LEVEL 2, CENTRAL PLAZA
Telephone: 353 500000 Telex: GOD
Directors: GOD (Managing, Sales, Financial)

Dear Mr. Cheeseberger,

Re: Creation Of The World

I very much regret that the strike which has stopped
production on the site for the last six days is still
continuing. In fact, it now shows every sign of becoming
rather ferocious as both sides become all the more
militant. I myself was today jostled and jeered by
a group of angry workmen under the title of 'The Creation
Workers Liberation Front' and, had it not been for my
judo training, I might not still be here to tell the
tale.

Meanwhile, we have been attracting no little attention
from the Press. Needless to say, certain misinformed
reporters in the more popular tabloids have taken what
I consider to be a biased attitude towards the dispute,
which I must say I find particularly offensive. I do,
however, believe we have fared slightly better with the
more informed journals which have at least seen fit to
publish our account of things. I fear though that this
has been an expensive exercise. Freedom of the Press
is certainly not cheap these days and I shall shortly
be submitting the invoices for my expenses to prove it.

I am enclosing herewith a sample of cuttings for your
reference.

Yours sincerely,

Veronica Makepiece

pp God

P.S.
Glad to hear Mr. Cohen-Cohen's health is improving, but
alarmed to learn he is planning to return to work shortly.
Do you think this is wise, under the present circumstances?

Enclosures

DEADLOCK REMAINS

Hardiman Twitcher
Industrial Correspondent

MANAGEMENT and workers on the World
Project were today as firmly as ever locked in
dispute when talks eventually broke up this evening. Little progress would appear to have been
made, with each side blaming the other for the
apparent deadlock.

The management are calling for an immediate return
to work by all workers while talks continue. The unions
are now calling for 43 days of rest a month, a 23-minute
working day, and a new bonus scheme. The manage
has offered the workers an extra half-da
decade and a 17-hour working d
lunch).

SEX SEX SEX

THERE WAS NO SIGN of any sex at all on
the picket-line outside The World today as
workers continued their industrial action. The
dispute, which some

DISPUTE DRAGS ON

AS the dispute at The World project dragged on today, there came news that the workers might decide
whether to reconvene earlier talks by the sub-committee
reporting to the permanent com-
wide special reports.

NO SIGNS OF PEACE

NO SIGNS of peace could be found on the
picket-line outside The World today as the
workers were described as 'insensitive and un-
caring' by their employers.

A spokesman for the workers told me that they
were not prepared to sta

PICKETS

Secondary picketing at The
World today reached epic pro
portions as over 500,000 men
joined the striking workers in a
show of strength. This "Day of
Action", called to sho
pathy of fello
downt

MANAGEMENT RUSE

A management ruse to employ
non-union labour in a bid to
complete the work on the ill-
fated World Project failed
disastrously today when the new
non-union workforce employed
he management decided to
not to continue work in the
of mounting threats from
unions.

was always a potentially
rdous scheme and likely to
e much ill-feeling and
tment. A management
esman branded the strikers
olent hooligans who had
overstepped th

FASCIST THUGS

THE WORKERS now on 24-hour-a-
day picket-duty outside the Creation
Project were today branded 'louts,
hooligans and complete tits' by Sir
Hugo Whippem. Sir Hugo, leader of
the 'Kick 'em In The Goolies' Party,
called upon the 'stupid, ignorant

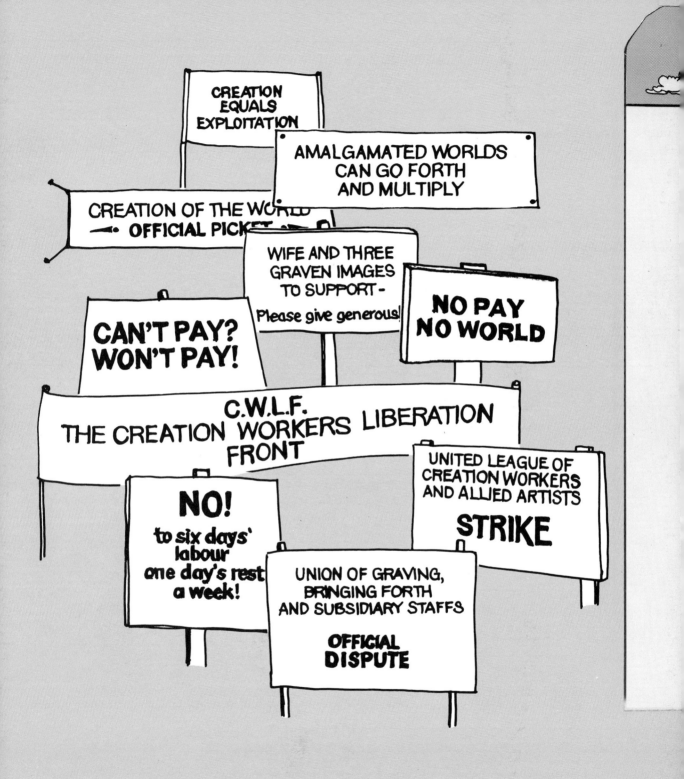

"GOD"

CREATIVE CONSULTANCY PROPERTY SERVICING
Agent for: AMALGAMATED WORLDS Pty.

Registered Office: UNIT 4, LEVEL 2, CENTRAL PLAZA
Telephone: 353 500000 Telex: GOD
Directors: GOD (Managing, Sales, Financial)

Dear Mr. Cohen-Cohen,

Re: Creation Of The World

I'm glad to know you are now fit and well again. I believe
Mr. Cheeseberger has brought you up to date with the
situation on the above, and I'm glad to be able to report
what may be cheering news.

We had an illuminating talk yesterday with our accountants,
who informed us of a novel loophole they have recently
discovered in the law that allows, under certain limited
circumstances, for a strike to be declared a tax loss which
can be offset against any tax payable in a given year.

The implication is that the strike may ironically turn out
to be financially beneficial to the company and will earn
us more than sufficient money to pay any and all of the
workers' demands. The accountants are still looking into
this area which they do point out is a legal minefield and
which will involve declaring the world a 'Non-Profit-
making House Association' for the first six months of use.
It will also involve a declaration that all animals and
beasts are bona fide members of one family.

I will report again shortly.

Yours optimistically,

Veronica Makepiece

God

"GOD"

CREATIVE CONSULTANCY PROPERTY SERVICING
Agent for: AMALGAMATED WORLDS Pty.
Registered Office: UNIT 4, LEVEL 2, CENTRAL PLAZA
Telephone: 353 500000 Telex: GOD
Directors: GOD (Managing, Sales, Financial)

Dear Mr. Cohen-Cohen,

As we had hoped, the accountants have been able to make use
of the considerable legal loophole referred to in my previous
letter and we are now thankfully approaching an end to the
dispute.

Unfortunately, due to some legal formality about which I am
not too clear, we now have to ensure the strike lasts for
a minimum of forty-one consecutive days. Since we are now on
the thirty-sixth day it was ironical that the workmen should
have chosen this of all days to throw in the towel and return
to work. Needless to say, we have resisted this move in order
to retain the large financial benefit to be gained from a
lengthy tax-deductable strike. We have therefore stated that
under no circumstances can we take the workers back, and have
set out new stringent terms which I feel sure they will turn
down. In this way, we hope to be able to avoid any settlement
for at least the next five days.

Yours deviously,

Veronica Makepiece

PP. God

"god"

CREATIVE CONSULTANCY PROPERTY SERVICING
Agent for: AMALGAMATED WORLDS Pty.
Registered Office: UNIT 4, LEVEL 2, CENTRAL PLAZA
Telephone: 353 500000 Telex: GOD
Directors: GOD (Managing, Sales, Financial)

Dear Mr. Cohen-Cohen,

Two days to go to the end of the dispute, and misfortune
has struck again. Just when we looked set for the tax dodge
to come our way, the workers have let us down by accepting
our new terms! They are at this moment preparing to return
to work and my only chance is to insist on further clauses.
But it will be difficult. Already we have reduced the workers'
wages to virtually nil with just one day's rest a month. I
will use my best endeavours but must warn you that, unless
we are very lucky, it does look as though the strike may be
all over within the hour.

Yours pessimistically,

Veronica Makepiece

"god"

CREATIVE CONSULTANCY PROPERTY SERVICING
Agent for: AMALGAMATED WORLDS Pty.
Registered Office: UNIT 4, LEVEL 2, CENTRAL PLAZA
Telephone: 353 500000 Telex: GOD
Directors: GOD (Managing, Sales, Financial)

Dear Mr. Cohen-Cohen,

We've done it! The workforce was practically suicidal in
its desire to return to work and I dare say we could not
have held out a day longer. But it matters not, because our
forty-one days are up and we have just this moment negotiated
for the workers to return to their tasks by lunchtime (whilst
we pocket a very tidy sum, courtesy of the Universal Government,
in the process).

I cannot tell you what a relief it is to have the whole
incident safely behind us for, although we have achieved
rich pickings in the face of adversity, it was not an episode
I would care to repeat. In addition, we are now a further
41 days behind schedule.

Nevertheless, we are now 'back on the rails', so to speak. And
far richer in the process.

Yours affluently,

Veronica Makepiece

pp. God

CREATIVE CONSULTANCY PROPERTY SERVICING
Agent for: AMALGAMATED WORLDS Pty.
Registered Office: UNIT 4, LEVEL 2, CENTRAL PLAZA
Telephone: 353 500000 Telex: GOD
Directors: GOD (Managing, Sales, Financial)

Dear Mr. Cohen-Cohen,

Re: Creation of The World

It is with very great pleasure that I am able to confirm that, apart from the installation of man and woman, the world is now finished. Perhaps you would care to visit the site, say tomorrow lunchtime, to see the finished article? I would be delighted to show you around.

I am sorry the project has taken so long, but I'm sure that when you see the final thing you will agree it was worth waiting.

Yours cheerfully,

Veronica Makepie

PP God

---

112 GOD G
123498 CONU G

ATTN: GOD

PLEASED TO REPORT WORLD V.V.V. NEARLY COMPLETE.
APART FROM ASSEMBLY AND INSTALLATION OF MAN AND
WOMAN HAVE PRACTICALLY FINISHED. ESTIMATE WE
WILL FINISH TOMORROW LUNCHTIME AT LATEST.

CAN WE HAVE MONEY?

REGARDS

TED SLAGWORTHY

123498 CONU G
112 GOD G

```
112 GOD G
234987 AMALWORLDS G
0001/AB

ATTN: GOD

YOUR LATEST LETTER INDICATES IMMINENT COMPLETION OF WORLD
PROJECT.
FRANKLY HIGHLY SCEPTICAL!
HAVE HEARD IT ALL BEFORE.
SOUNDS TO ME LIKE ANOTHER PIECE OF WISHFUL THINKING.
NOT AT ALL SURE I BELIEVE A WORD YOU SAY.
WITHHOLDING ANY COMMENT AT THIS STAGE!

T.G. COHEN-COHEN

234987 AMALWORLDS G
112 GOD G
```

COSMIC & UNIVERSAL CONSTRUCTION CO.
General Builders & Contractors

3rd Arch Along
Limepit Viaduct
Telephone 18194804612 (one line)
Telex CONU

MEMBER OF THE FEDERATION OF SMALL BUILDERS
AND BUILDING CONTRACTORS

Dear God,

Re: Creation of The World

You will recall from our last conversation concerning the above that we had only a relatively minor matter to attend to, namely the manufacture, assembly and installation of man and woman. However, I very much regret to report that we have suffered a number of problems with this work.

Our first trouble was caused when the manufacturers informed us that they had lost the photographs you had supplied from which they were to work. Not wishing to upset you or cause you unnecessary trouble, we sent them a few sketches that we executed ourselves. We also provided a few additional details over the phone. However, I'm afraid the results were not perhaps quite what we had anticipated. Apart from a rather upsetting grin and a complete lack of hair, the man and woman they manufactured also turned out to be mechanically unsound and totally impossible to control, even with the remote-control walkie-talkies provided.

We also found the leg mechanism rather difficult to assemble, with the result that the man and woman kept falling over. In the end I'm afraid we were forced to affix casters to their feet, which certainly cured the problem but did lead to a slightly ungainly way of walking.

After that things went from bad to worse. Neither the man nor the woman's head would balance on their shoulders and kept rolling off, their hearts developed a habit of whining at low speed and their tongues overheated and caught fire. The arms were found to be defective and had to be replaced. The legs were too short and had to have wooden attachments added to bring them up to the lengths detailed in the specifications. In addition, we discovered the ears had rust spots and were coming away from their fixing bolts, and the mechanism for eating would operate only at a very fast speed.

We had hoped to iron out these problems and bring the man and woman round for you to see, and indeed only last Thursday we set off with them to visit you. However, we were less than two light years into our journey when there was a terrible smell of burning and the man's left leg burst into flames. (We later diagnosed it as a wiring fault and have now rewired both bodies and installed a sprinkler system in each.)

Finally, we have discovered that the wings which we had hoped to incorporate for flying are somewhat impractical and we have therefore decided to disregard the 'flight' specifications. We are sure you will approve of this slight modification, particularly since it will allow us to complete the work more rapidly.

I enclose herewith our new designs and trust that they meet with your full approval.

Yours unfortunately,

Gwyn MacTaggart (Secretary)

p̸ Ted Slagworthy
For Cosmic & Universal Construction Co.

112 GOD G
123498 CONU G

ATTN: GOD

HAVE DISCOVERED MAN'S BRAIN FITTED WRONG WAY ROUND. HE'S
NOW WALKING AND TALKING BACKWARDS. REPLACEMENT BRAIN ON
ORDER.

HIS EYES NOT WORKING CORRECTLY EITHER AND AS A RESULT HAS
HAD A NUMBER OF RATHER SERIOUS ACCIDENTS WHICH HAVE PUT US
BACK SLIGHTLY.

ALSO SERIOUS IMBALANCE IN DIGESTIVE SYSTEM. HEAVY-DUTY FACE
MASKS AND RESPIRATORS ON ORDER ... MUST DASH, CAN HEAR HIM
COMING.

TED SLAGWORTHY

123498 CONU G
112 GOD G

---

112 GOD G
123498 CONU G

ATTN: GOD

NOW FITTED MAN'S REPLACEMENT BRAIN. DIGESTIVE SYSTEM NOW
FUNCTIONING PROPERLY, THANK GOODNESS. EYES IMPROVING.

NEW PROBLEM, HOWEVER ... WOMAN UNABLE TO STOP WHISTLING.
QUITE PLEASANT FOR FIRST FIVE MINUTES, BUT NOW UNBEARABLE.
HAVE TRIED STICKING PLASTER, BUT TO NO EFFECT. HAVE
ALSO TRIED LARGE HAMMER, WHICH HAD SLIGHTLY MORE EFFECT.
IS REGAINING CONSCIOUSNESS NOW, AND AM CONSIDERING REMOVAL
OF HER TEETH. IT'S OUR LAST HOPE.

---

112 GOD G
123498 CONU G

ATTN: GOD

HAVE CURED ALL PROBLEMS. WOMAN STOPPED WHISTLING. BOTH
MAN AND WOMAN NOW WALKING/TALKING/EATING AS REQUIRED.

AM PREPARING TO TAKE BOTH ON ROAD TEST.

WILL REPORT.

TED SLAGWORTH

123498 CONU G
112 GOD G

---

112 GOD G
123498 CONU G

ATTN: GOD

ROAD TEST ON MAN NOT TOO SUCCESSFUL. HE'S UNABLE TO
NEGOTIATE SHARP CORNERS. CANNOT GO UPHILL. AFRAID
TO GO INTO REVERSE.

ALSO TENDS TO LIMP BADLY, ESPECIALLY AFTER WALKING
INTO BOLLARDS. (ALSO COMPLAINS A LOT, ESPECIALLY
AFTER WALKING INTO BOLLARDS. AND NOW SINGS SOPRANO.)

ADJUSTMENTS NOW BEING MADE.

TED SLAGWORTHY

123498 CONU G
112 GOD G

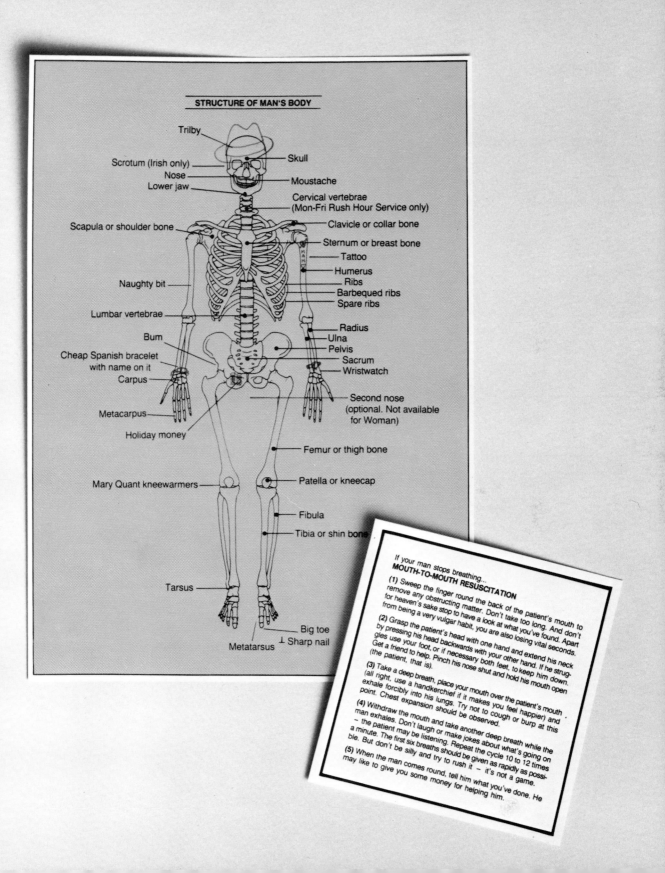

STRUCTURE OF MAN'S BODY

Trilby

Scrotum (Irish only)
Nose
Lower jaw

Skull
Moustache

Cervical vertebrae
(Mon-Fri Rush Hour Service only)

Scapula or shoulder bone

Clavicle or collar bone

Sternum or breast bone

Tattoo

Humerus

Ribs

Naughty bit

Barbequed ribs

Spare ribs

Lumbar vertebrae

Radius

Bum

Ulna

Pelvis

Cheap Spanish bracelet
with name on it

Sacrum

Wristwatch

Carpus

Metacarpus

Second nose
(optional. Not available
for Woman)

Holiday money

Femur or thigh bone

Mary Quant kneewarmers

Patella or kneecap

Fibula

Tibia or shin bone

Tarsus

Big toe
⊥ Sharp nail

Metatarsus

If your man stops breathing...
MOUTH-TO-MOUTH RESUSCITATION

(1) Sweep the finger round the back of the patient's mouth to remove any obstructing matter. Don't take too long. And don't for heaven's sake stop to have a look at what you've found. Apart from being a very vulgar habit, you are also losing vital seconds.

(2) Grasp the patient's head with one hand and extend his neck by pressing his head backwards with your other hand. If he struggles use your foot, or if necessary both feet, to keep him down. Get a friend to help. Pinch his nose shut and hold his mouth open (the patient, that is).

(3) Take a deep breath, place your mouth over the patient's mouth (all right, use a handkerchief if it makes you feel happier) and exhale forcibly into his lungs. Try not to cough or burp at this point. Chest expansion should be observed.

(4) Withdraw the mouth and take another deep breath while the man exhales. Don't laugh or make jokes about what's going on – the patient may be listening. Repeat the cycle 10 to 12 times a minute. The first six breaths should be given as rapidly as possible. But don't be silly and try to rush it – it's not a game.

(5) When the man comes round, tell him what you've done. He may like to give you some money for helping him.

FRACTURES
What to do if your Man or Woman should suffer a fracture

Arm and shoulder If the elbow can be flexed without increasing the pain, place the forearm across the chest and apply a sling. Should flexion be too painful, use a large piece of iron piping and a sharp stick to quieten the patient down.

Leg Gently pull the uninjured leg to rest against the injured one and place pads or a padded splint between the legs. Be careful — there are a few delicate bits around the top end. With scarves, bandages or any old bits of string or thick rope, tie the feet and knees together above and below the site of the fracture. Gag the patient. Run off with his/her money.

Pelvis A broad folded cloth may be placed around the pelvis to give support or just to keep the patient flat. Don't make rude remarks about the size of the patient's optional second nose (applicable in Man only) at this stage. A doctor will do this later if he feels it is necessary.

Spine When injury to the spine is suspected, do not move the patient until there is a stretcher available and a sufficient number of helpers to aid you. Place pads on the stretcher for the neck, lumbar curve, and ankles. Also place books and magazines on the stretcher in case the patient fancies something to read. And place a few sandwiches and crisps on the stretcher in case he or she is a bit peckish.

HOME MAINTENANCE OF YOU
Some common problems and how

Problem	Cause
Will not breathe	Dead
	Practically dead
	Joined Tory Party
Burning smells	Forgot to put out cigarette
	Spontaneous combustion
	Too many Indian meals
Ignition warning light stays on above idle speed	Broken or slipping fanbelt
	No generator output
	Hernia
Won't get out of bed in the morning	Hangover
	On the skive
	Dead
Constipation	Clogged vent in fuel filler c
	Too many bran tablets
Pain in groin	Excess fuel/over-rich mixtu
	Rupture

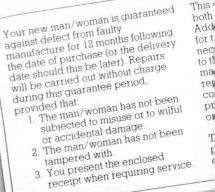

Guarant

Your new man/woman is guaranteed against defect from faulty manufacture for 12 months following the date of purchase (or the delivery date should this be later). Repairs will be carried out without charge during this guarantee period, provided that:

1. The man/woman has not been subjected to misuse or to wilful or accidental damage.
2. The man/woman has not been tampered with.
3. You present the enclosed receipt when requiring service.

N OR WOMAN
with them

Remedy
Call undertaker
Dry with clean cloth or spray with a moisture repellant
Call mental hospital
Allow to cool and adjust
Check brain terminals and quickly fill bucket with water
Allow to cool/Open window/Open ice-cool lager
Call doctor
Check security of leads to generator
Tighten up or renew
Top up and try again
Call his/her employer and tell lies
Change sheets
Clear vent with pin and wire
Clear vent with rake and pitchfork
Turn engine on starter with accelerator fully depressed. If this does not clear excess, remove sparking plugs, dry and replace
Check and tighten nuts

...ee covers the cost of
...ls and labour.
..., there will be no charge
...t where it is found
...o return the man/woman
...shops for repair. If your
...an has to be removed for
...imilar man/woman of
...le shape and size will be
... for the period that the
...s out of service.

...rantee is, of course, wi...
...e to your statutory or
...n law rights.

BREAKDOWN OF YOUR MAN OR WOMAN
Precautions and Cure

Daily check (or before a journey)
Check for damage to legs, eyes, ears. Check alcohol and tobacco levels. Top up as necessary.

Weekly check
Check the stomach to make sure it is full. If not, top up as necessary. Check the lungs to make sure they are still operating. Check both the ears to make sure they're clean. If not, use a damp rag and a little turps. Comb the hair. Brush the teeth. Check all underwear.

Checks on the move
Take careful note of any unusual behaviour or excessive noise. If this occurs, investigate before continuing your journey.

MAN
Specifications

Size:	6 ft 2 in (adjustable)
Weight:	148 lb
Turning circle:	18 in
Turning circle (on 8 pints):	96 ft
Acceleration:	0-4 mph in 23 seconds
Maximum speed:	8 mph
Fuel consumption:	3 square meals a day
Lubrication:	Watneys Red Barrel

Factory fitted extras:

Push button radio	*Available*
Alloy wheels	No
Halogen headlights	No
Sunroof	No
Fig leaf apron	No
Sideburns	Yes
Tattoos	Yes
Twin carburettors	Yes
Anti-dazzle mirror	Yes
Rear wash-wipe	No
Automatic transmission	No
Wing mirrors	No
Aerial	No
Arms	Yes
Legs	Yes
Scales	Yes
Gills	No
Tail	No
Tool kit	No
Tool	No
	Yes

CREATIVE CONSULTANCY PROPERTY SERVICING
Agent for: AMALGAMATED WORLDS Pty.
Registered Office: UNIT 4, LEVEL 2, CENTRAL PLAZA
Telephone: 353 500000 Telex: GOD
Directors: GOD (Managing, Sales, Financial)

Dear Mr. Slagworthy,

Re: Creation Of The World

On my instructions, the overseer has provided a full
report on progress, a copy of which I enclose herewith.
You will recall that you informed me that all the work
was complete. I would suggest that the enclosed is at
considerable variance with this.

Perhaps you would clarify.

Yours dubiously,

Veronica Makepiece

PP. God

Enclosure

REPORT ON THE CONTINUED CONSTRUCTION OF

THE WORLD

I was asked by the client, Mr God, to report on the construction of the a

property which has recently been built and which the constructing agent ha

intimated was now complete.

I would report thus:

1.) On the whole the property was in a sound condition. Considerable
work had been done to all facing elements and I was impressed
by the level of services provided. Following this, however, I
would advise that certain features still require attention:

a.) A number of cracks and fractures were in evidence, where portions
of the Shelf (Continental) appears to have slipped after installation. This was particularly evident in the San Andreas region.
I would suggest that these cracks be raked out thoroughly and all
loose and friable material removed. All cracks should be pinned
with metal joist pins and the gap filled with a suitable sand/
cement/mortar (3.1.1).

b.) I found evidence of spillage along many coastlines, with severe
damage in many parts. I suggest a retaining wall be constructed
in these areas to prevent further spillage.

c.) A number of countries showed evidence of damp patches due to
insufficient preparation and it is my recommendation that these
areas be removed and treated by an accredited firm of damp-proof
specialists using preparatory brand materials.

d.) There is evidence of settlement having occurred throughout the
property. Geological features are bowed and out of true and
there appears to have been fracturing and folding, giving an
unsightly appearance to many upland areas. It is my recommendation that these be removed and the areas again be filled in
with a level sand and cement base that would allow rainwater to
drain off without blockage.

e.) Electrical tests placed upon bedrock surfaces revealed extensive
evidence of rising dampness throughout and, although this may
be attributable in part to defective rainwater channels, I feel
it is essential that a reputable firm of specialists be instructed who will thereafter issue a 20-year guarantee.

f.) Externally the decorative state of the property is still poor and
in need of attention.

g.) No comment as to the function of the sanitaryware can be made, as
the water was turned off at the time of my inspection.

h.) There are **two** prepayment gas meters within the property which would
suggest that originally it may have been intended for occupation
as two partially separate habitations. No test was placed on the
gas installations, this being the province of a specialist.

112 GOD G
123498 CONU G

ATTN: GOD

DELIGHTED TO REPORT THAT WORLD IS AT LONG LAS[
COMPLETE = REPEAT WORLD COMPLETE!

KINDEST REGARDS.

TED SLAGWORTHY

123498 CONU G
112 GOD G

ATTN: TED SLAGWORTHY

HAVE YOU BEEN HITTING THE BOTTLE? AM I DREAMING?
CAN IT BE TRUE?

PLEASE CONFIRM YOUR LATEST TELEX WAS NOT A CRUEL
JOKE. IS WORLD REALLY COMPLETE?

GOD

112 GOD G
123498 CONU G

ATTN: GOD

PREVIOUS TELEX QUITE CORRECT. YOUR SCEPTICISM UNDER-
STANDABLE. CAN HARDLY BELIEVE IT MYSELF.

TED

112 GOD G
123498 CONU G

ATTN: GOD

FURTHER TO YOUR REQUEST THAT I VISIT SITE TO CONFIRM
EARLIER REPORTS AND TO ENSURE THE SLIPPERY LITTLE
TOADS WEREN'T LYING, AM AT SITE AND IT'S ALL TRUE!
WORK REALLY IS FINISHED.

WILD PARTY NOW IN PROGRESS ... MUST GO.

VERONICA MAKEPI[

234987 AMALWORLDS G
112 GOD G
0001/AB

ATTN: T.G. COHEN-COHEN

ECSTATIC TO REPORT THAT WORLD IS FINALLY COMPLETE, DOWN
TO THE VERY LAST DETAIL. HAVE CHECKED, RECHECKED AND
DOUBLE-CHECKED THAT THIS IS SO.

CHAMPAGNE TO FOLLOW.

KINDEST REGARDS.

GOD

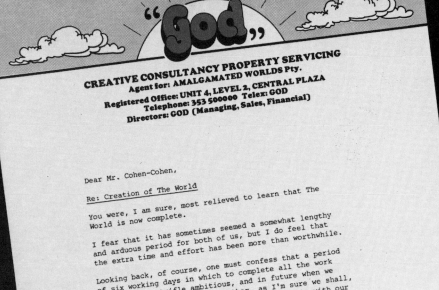

"God"

CREATIVE CONSULTANCY PROPERTY SERVICING
Agent for: AMALGAMATED WORLDS Pty.
Registered Office: UNIT 4, LEVEL 2, CENTRAL PLAZA
Telephone: 353 500000 Telex: GOD
Directors: GOD (Managing, Sales, Financial)

Dear Mr. Cohen-Cohen,

Re: Creation of The World

You were, I am sure, most relieved to learn that The World is now complete.

I fear that it has sometimes seemed a somewhat lengthy and arduous period for both of us, but I do feel that the extra time and effort has been more than worthwhile.

Looking back, of course, one must confess that a period of six working days in which to complete all the work was perhaps a trifle ambitious, and in future when we come to create new worlds together, as I'm sure we shall, I suggest we perhaps be a little more realistic with our schedules. I think, too, that we might perhaps have allowed our enthusiasm to run away with us on one or two other aspects, notably the man and woman.

However, I'm sure that we won't let the few upsetting incidents along the way mar the many, many hours of happiness which the project has given us, and I for one will be a much sadder person now that it is over.

I trust that you and your wife will call in at my office when you are next in this area. I would be delighted to see you both and to take you out for a spot of lunch.

With my most sincere regards,

God

TOTAL

MIC & UNIVERSAL CONSTRUCTION CO.
General Builders & Contractors

3rd Arch Along
Limepit Viaduct
Telephone 18194804612 (one line)
Telex CONU

MEMBER OF THE FEDERATION OF SMALL BUILDERS
AND BUILDING CONTRACTORS

Dear God,

Re: Creation of The World

Please find enclosed our invoice for the work completed on the
above project. As you will see, we have itemised the various costs
involved. The final amount is slightly more than we had originally
estimated but I am sure you will agree the costs are realistic,
bearing in mind the amount of work involved.

I trust you will find the costs to your satisfaction and will
arrange for a speedy settlement.

Would it be possible for a cheque to be sent by return of post?

With kindest regards,

Gwyn MacTaggart (Secretary)

p.p Ted Slagworthy
Cosmic & Universal Construction Co.
(BUILDERS OF BRAND NEW WORLDS)

"God"

CREATIVE CONSULTANCY PROPERTY SERVICING
Agent for: AMALGAMATED WORLDS Pty.
Registered Office: UNIT 4, LEVEL 2, CENTRAL PLAZA
Telephone: 353 500000 Telex: GOD
Directors: GOD (Managing, Sales, Financial)

Dear Mr. Slagworthy,

Re: Creation Of The World

Thank you for your letter and invoice.

I regret that there is not the slightest prospect of
you receiving settlement in the foreseeable future.
Or even, for that matter, in the unforeseeable future.

May I remind you that the work you carried out was
late, poor, and totally in breach of all contracts you
signed.

I have no intention of even considering your invoice
until I return from holiday in six years' time, by
which time you can be assured that I will have forgotten
all about it.

I trust you will find this to your satisfaction.

Yours sarcastically,

CROOKED & BENT
Solicitors, Commissioners for Oaths, Licensed Betting Shop

Dear Mr. Slagworthy,

Re: Creation Of The World

As you no doubt remember, we act as solicitors
for Mr. God and have been asked by him to supply you
with the enclosed 980-page legal resume. I would
be grateful if you would read and return this to us,
together with any points you may wish to make. This
is essential to opening of negotiations regarding
settlement arising from works undertaken.

Failure to reply satisfactorily within two days
will be deemed as forfeiture of all your rights to
settlement.

Yours lawfully,

P.P. Scribbling

P.P. Scribbling (Partner)

```
                                  < 4
                       -4 2 5 1 6 3 7 2 2 8
               -0 5 7 4 6 2 8 2 0 1 8 5 7 6
       -9 4 8 5 7 1 0 2 9 4 8 5 7 6 8 4 1 6 3 7 2 8
4 4 7 5 8 6 9 2 0 3 9 0 4 9 5 7 2 8 1 2 4 3 5 5 4 7 6
9 4 8 5 7 2 9 6 8 4 7 5 6 3 9 5 8 3 7 5 6 2 0 0 0 9
756,476,831,298,354,587,683,509,352,546,657,233,441,552
```

(Gratuity not included)

NEW WORLD OPENS TO CRITICAL ACCLAIM

By Our Own Correspondent

The new world, commissioned by Amalgamated Worlds Pty, and built by the relatively unknown Cosmic & Universal Construction Co under the direction of Mr God, was today officially opened to the general public for the first time.

Looking far smaller than it had done in many of the publicity shots, it was immediately the subject of much professional scrutiny.

It has been built with an elliptical orbital structure and self-centring gravity and is certain to draw comparison with a number of other planets of similar design.

I personally found it comfortable to ride on, well appointed, and with good economical performance. However, there were a few complaints that the rotation could cause giddiness and a slight feeling of sickness

CALL ME ADAM

By Our Medical Correspondent

The launch of the new World today also saw the launch of an entirely new man and woman. Created with the modern need for stylish finish and economical performance, it was decided to adopt the conventional bipedal design of earlier models but to combine it with a new vertical posture and, in the case of man, an optional second nose. Of particular interest to many will be the new highly-powered brain that allows the man and woman to perform a number of complicated actions not previously possible in this type of body.

OH WHAT A SHAMBLES!

ALTHOUGH others stood and gawped in admiration at the new World, I could not share their enthusiasm. And as I reclined on some of the already crumbling geological features, I had the chance to reflect on this shambling monster that has taken so long to build and gone so far over budget that it has seen grown accountants crying softly into their ledgers.

But I for one will not object when the greatest white elephant of our times closes in the next few months, as I confidently predict it will. What can have possessed a company

IN THE GARDEN

Quentin Turnip

I was thrilled last night to see at last the launch of the new Garden of Eden. We have waited a long time to see anything as bold as this in the field of garden design and I personally take my wheelbarrow off to the imaginative planners who undertook the work.

The luxuriance and splendour is indeed a tribute to the many hours of careful thought and planning that have gone into this

IT'S OPEN!

THE curtains were drawn back for the first time last night on The World. At a lavish reception held to honour the occasion, a host of glittering celebrities paid tribute to the great endeavour that has bee

IT'S A WORLD

LAST NIGHT the champagne flowed like water, the revellers danced till they fell, and it wasn't till the first light of dawn that the celebrations showed any sign of abating.

Yes, this was a first night to end all first nights. And with good reason. We had all just witnessed that most momentous of events: the opening of a new World. Tomorrow, the crowds will flock to inspect the new pro- perty, but last night viewing was restricted to the chosen few: universal ambassadors, statesmen, interstellar dignitaries, sports and showbusiness celebrities, the crew of the Starship Enterprise... and of course the peo- ple who actually built the World.

And there to welcome th...

After I'd got him even more drunk and in- capable, I managed to wheedle still more juicy gossip out of Mr. Slagworthy, the "Cinderella of the Construction World" who wasn't invited to the launch last night.

He dished up the dirt all right. No holds were barred. In fact, the black magic scout- master (sorry, builder) even told me how he was nearly raped when he accepted a lift home from the newly-created woman.

When I revealed I was a News of the New World reporter, Mr. Slagworthy said he couldn't give a stuff, made his excuses and left.

OF MEN AND MOUNTAINS

As the light dropped a few stops yesterday evening, we came to pay tribute to a work of true genius. This was the most rare of occasions: an occasion when all the critics were unanimous in their praise. This was to be the event of the year as all gave their approval to the bra... new World.

WORLD WITHOUT END

Make no mistake – this is a world without end!

This is just the opportunity the galax- ies have been waiting for and we have to thank God for giving it to them. My only reservation is the time it took them to complete it. But now we've proved it can be done, let's go on and create another, and another, a...

World Gains

BRISK EARLY TRADING in shares of the newly created World produced rapid up- ward gains as the market clearly showed its approval of the new project.

Shares, which opened the day at 153.7, rose quickly to 159.7 as investors were quick to snap up the early issues. But a note of cau- tion, no doubt due to the generally depres- sed real-estates market, saw shares slide slightly before the close, to finish the day up raph! six at 153.8

I WAS THERE
Sun Exclusive

I was there and saw it all, *writes Sun reporter Ar- thur Pint.* It was an experience I will never forget and which will live with me forever. My only criticism is that there weren't enough girls.

Single Girl

Despite the lavish and sumptuous banquet laid on, the party atmosphere and all the razzamatazz, I couldn't find a single girl to photo-

Shame

It's a shame that on an occa- sion like this the public can't be given just the odd bit of skirt to cast their eyes over

Dear God,

    I am writing to ask whether something can't be done to stop
the large number of people using our road as a short cut on the
way to your world. This used to be a quiet street where the

Dear God,

    I thought you might like to know that your
new world appears to be leaking a rather nasty
brown liquid. In addition, my wife tells me

Dear God,

    I am writing to you in connection with your new world
which, I was alarmed to notice, appears to be emitting
dense clouds of black, pungent smoke. I hope that this is

Dear God,

    Recently I have noticed a strange smell which I
can only identify as coming from your new world, and
I am keen that you should visit the site as I am concerned that it may be toxic and could be polluting the

Dear Sir,

    This morning I was outraged to find a large
mountain in my back garden. It would appear to have
fallen off your world, and I insist that you call
round to remove the offending object immediately

                    Rory Simmin.

Dear Sir,

    My family was upset this morning to see a strange man
walking round our neighbourhood. He had a "head" and, strange
though it may seem, appeared to be walking on two legs, so I
can only assume that he was from your new world. I'd be grateful if you could ensure this sort of incident does not occur
again, as it only frightens the children and upsets the wife

                    S. Jimmy.